SMOOTHIE BOWLS

Eliq Maranik

SMOOTHIE BOWLS

Inspiring Healthy Foods

h.f.ullmann

Contents

Preface

Who can resist a bowl full of wholesome goodness, garnished with tantalizing toppings? I love regular smoothies, but I've also become a fan of smoothie bowls of late.

A smoothie bowl is a delicious, filling, and nutritious twist on classic "porridge," only containing extra ingredients and much more flavor. A smoothie bowl is ideal for breakfast, a snack, a quick lunch, or even a dessert—depending on what ingredients you use. It has a thicker consistency than a regular smoothie and contains more energy because it's packed with fiber, vitamins, minerals, antioxidants, and healthy fats. I usually use toppings to garnish it: homemade muesli and granola, fresh and dried berries or fruits, all kinds of nuts and seeds—even vegetables. A smoothie bowl should be thick enough to be eaten with a spoon.

The nice things about smoothie bowls are the variety of flavors and combinations, the fact that most ingredients keep well in the freezer or pantry, and the fact that you can make a smoothie bowl in less than five minutes. Say goodbye once and for all to those boring breakfasts: eat your fill, balance your body, and get the energy you need to cope with the demands of everyday life.

All the recipes in the book are raw, soy-free, and vegan. A small number of the recipes contain honey and/or bee pollen among the ingredients. Obviously, you can replace honey with agave syrup or drop the bee pollen completely. These days, stores offer plenty of alternatives to dairy products on their shelves and, indeed, the supply has never been more abundant. Nor has the demand. If you wish, you can also use "regular" dairy.

Treat yourself to a tastier and healthier life. Your body will reward you—your digestion will work perfectly, your energy levels will become far more balanced, and you'll be much happier and more stable. Happy people spread joy.

Eliq Maranik

Ingredients

Consider buying organic and raw as much as possible. That way, your food will retain all the goodness that was in it from the start. Find out more about berries, fruit, and vegetables on pages 17–18.

Below is a handy guide to various ingredients you should have at home:

FROZEN FRUIT and BERRIES: Banana, blueberries, cherries, dates, kiwi, mango, melon, nectarines, papaya, peaches, pineapple, plums, raspberries, strawberries, and all kinds of berries freeze well. Apples, citrus fruits, pears, and watermelon are best frozen as juice.

FRESH FRUIT: All fresh fruits make a fine smoothie bowl, but, for best consistency, use frozen fruit and berries. That way, you won't have to use ice, which impairs flavor.

VEGETABLES: You can "smuggle" avocado, beets, carrots, celery, kale, pumpkin, spinach, zucchini, and many other vegetables into a smoothie bowl. Go easy in the beginning, taste your way forward, and make sure you don't use too many vegetables.

NUTS: Preferably, choose natural, unsalted, organic, raw, unroasted almonds, Brazil nuts, hazelnuts, pecans, pine nuts, pistachios, and walnuts. Nuts go rancid fairly quickly, so if you don't use nuts in large quantities, freeze them instead. Most nuts benefit from prior soaking, anywhere from a couple of hours to overnight, which removes indigestible enzymes. Pre-soaking will also ensure that your body absorbs more nutrients from nuts.

NUT and SEED BUTTER: Raw, preferably organic, nut butters are a good source of energy and rich in both minerals and protein. Nut butters made of roasted nuts are not as nutritious, so go for raw on principle. Almond butter, cashew butter, hazelnut butter, peanut butter, pistachio butter, tahini (sesame paste), walnut butter, and many others are available in health food stores. Nut butters are not difficult to make at home and can be flavored with raw cacao, cinnamon, vanilla, and other goodies.

SEEDS: Chia seeds, flaxseed, hemp seeds, psyllium seeds, pumpkin seeds, sesame seeds, and sunflower seeds make a perfect addition to smoothie bowls. Besides, chia seeds, flaxseed, and psyllium seeds form a gel that provides a thicker consistency.

PROTEIN: Brown rice protein, hemp protein, oat protein, pea protein, and many other great vegan protein mixes are available in health food stores. Find out more about protein on page 23.

HEALTHY OILS: To get the most out of oils, make sure you buy them cold-pressed. They're sometimes called extra virgin or raw oils. Preferably, buy organic. Almond oil, coconut oil, and nut oils, avocado oil, canola oil, chia seed oil, flaxseed oil, hempseed oil, and olive oil, as well as many others are available in supermarkets and/or health food stores. Oil goes rancid relatively quickly, so it's wise to buy small bottles. Flaxseed oil and hempseed oil should be stored in a refrigerator, while other oils are best kept in a cool, dark place.

FIBER: Psyllium seeds and psyllium husks, flax seeds, chia seeds.

SUPERFOODS: Baobab, barley grass, bee pollen (not for vegans), beet powder, buckwheat (sprouted), cacao butter, cacao nibs and raw cacao, camu camu, carob, carrot powder, cayenne pepper, chia seeds, chlorella, cinnamon, coconut (unsweetened, grated), coconut sugar, ginger, goji berries, hemp seeds, inca berries, lúcuma, maca, mulberries, spirulina, stinging nettle, turmeric, vanilla powder, vegan proteins, wheatgrass.

SUPERBERRY and FRUIT POWDERS: Berry powders are usually made of whole freeze-dried berries, including pulp, skin, and seeds, which have been ground to a powder. As always, I recommend that you buy organic and raw before other options. Watch out for sweetened berry powders! Berry powder is very convenient because it keeps up to 18 months. In addition, most powders freeze well if you want to keep them for longer. The powders on offer are many and varied, e.g. açaí, acerola, aronia, blackberry, blackcurrant, blueberry, buckthorn, cloudberry, cranberry, goji berry, guarana, inca berry, lúcuma, mango, maqui, moringa, mulberry, passion fruit, pomegranate, raspberry, rosehip, sour cherry, strawberry, etc.

SWEETENERS: Agave syrup, banana powder and frozen bananas, coconut, coconut sugar, dates, maple syrup, raw honey (not vegan), stevia, and sweet fruits.

LIQUIDS: Water, fresh juices, coconut water, almond, seed, and nut milks, oat and soy products.

Selecting and using a blender

Before investing in a blender, make sure you're clear about what you need. Buying a relatively inexpensive model may prove to be the wrong choice and so, for that matter, might be an expensive one. What's particularly annoying is blowing money on a blender that doesn't meet your expectations and then banishing it to the back of the kitchen cabinet. In this section, I provide some tips about the points to consider before buying a new blender.

FREQUENCY AND QUANTITY: If you're planning on making smoothies frequently, it definitely pays to invest in a high-speed blender. High-speed blenders are durable, come with a long warranty and can basically blend anything to a silky consistency—from ice, seeds, nuts, frozen fruit and berries to hard vegetables, such as carrots and beets, and all kinds of leafy greens. They're fast and efficient. They do the job perfectly, without any ingredients getting stuck or failing to engage with the blade. Some brands come with an optional dry-blending jar, which allows you to make your own flour from various grains, soy beans, or nuts/seeds.

PRICE: Blender prices range from a relatively modest cost to a substantial investment, and they vary in quality. There are basic blenders for making simple liquid smoothies and there are high-speed ones for making more advanced smoothies and smoothie bowls, such as those containing ice, frozen fruit, hard vegetables, seeds, and nuts, and those for making nut milks.

DIFFERENT SPEEDS: It's important that your blender can work at different speeds. Usually starting on a low speed in order to crush and blend the contents, you then increase the speed in order to make the smoothie homogenous and creamy. Finally, you let the blender run on a high speed for a short time. Vitamix Pro 750 offers several preset programs, which is ideal if you want to do other things while the blender is working.

MOTOR POWER: Naturally, it's important that your blender has a robust motor in order to crush ice cubes and frozen ingredients, among other reasons. The motor should have a minimum power output of 1,000 watts, and preferably more.

CONTAINER DESIGN is important for proper flow during the blending process. The container should never be perfectly round, but have a shape that creates resistance. That's why most quality blenders come with square or clover-leaf-shaped containers. The container's top lid should have a filler cap with a feed hole for adding new ingredients during blending, without having to stop the blender or open the lid entirely.

Containers made of BPA-free, unbreakable and scratch-resistant plastic offer an additional advantage. Glass containers are good, but they are usually very heavy and break more easily. Jars made of inexpensive plastic may contain BPA, and they may scratch and discolor easily. If you go for a simpler machine, I recommend buying one with a glass jar.

BLADES should be large, sturdy, and twisted at the right angle. Use a wooden spoon or a flexible silicone spatula when emptying the container or stirring the contents so as not to damage the blade. Never use metal objects inside the jar.

ACCOMPANYING TAMPER: A good blender comes with an accompanying tamper, which is used to push the ingredients down toward the blade. The tamper is tailored to the jar and doesn't damage the metal blade. Use the tamper to feed hard or slow-moving ingredients down toward the blade and remove any air pockets. Containers come in different sizes, so never use a tamper in a machine for which it isn't intended, even it they're the same brand. Always read the instructions carefully or contact your dealer if there's anything you're not sure about. *Never, ever* feed anything into a blender that doesn't come with an accompanying tamper while the blender is running!

PROTECTION AGAINST OVERHEATING: Some machines are equipped with a built-in overheat protection mechanism. The machine simply stops and you have to wait some time before being able to use it again.

WARRANTY is another thing to bear in mind. I've owned a dozen or so blenders, roughly half of which broke down within a year. Check the warranty period before buying a blender. The standard period is one year, or two years if you're lucky. The blenders I'm using come with a seven-year warranty.

LOOK AFTER YOUR BLENDER: Read the instructions carefully or contact your dealer if there's anything you're not sure about. The warranty won't apply if you misuse the blender, so look after it.

Common beginners' mistakes

» dropping the container on the floor, causing it to crack and break.
» damaging the blade with sharp or metal objects when scraping out food.
» poking things into the machine with the motor running.
» placing the container incorrectly onto the machine.
» removing the container before the machine has stopped, even with the motor switched off.
» using ice or ingredients that are too hard (in the more basic models).
» causing the motor to overheat.

Things to keep in mind when buying a blender

» price.

» motor power output (at least 1,000 W).

» number of speeds.

» preset programs.

» material, size, and form of the container.

» design and thickness of the blade.

» whether it has a tamper and filler cap.

» whether it has protection against overheating.

» warranty period.

All the recipes in this book were made with the Vitamix Pro 750 and Vitamix S-30 high-speed blenders, both of which have an accompanying tamper to make the job easier. There's a definite advantage to having a high-speed blender when making smoothie bowls, because you will commonly use nuts, seeds, and green leaves, as well as frozen ingredients.

Vitamix Pro 750 is a true powerhouse! It's a largish blender with a 2-quart / 2-liter container (though you can buy smaller containers separately). Vitamix S-30, also called *personal blender*, is a smaller machine with a 1¼-quart / 1.2-liter container and a takeout container, much like a sports drink container in which you can blend ingredients directly. You fill it with the ingredients of your choice, screw on the blade base, attach it to the blender, run the blender to achieve the desired consistency, and then replace the base with an accompanying sports drink lid. It's perfect for taking into work, for when you're working out, or for when you're on your way somewhere.

If you don't have a high-speed blender but wish to use frozen fruit, let it thaw slightly and use more liquid than indicated in the recipe—or just drop the ice altogether if your blender can't handle it. If the ingredients get stuck or aren't engaging with the blade, stop the machine, scrape the sides of the jar with a silicone spatula, and then just run the blender again.

When making smoothies, always add the liquid first, then the soft ingredients that are easy to crush, then the nuts or seeds, and frozen fruit or ice last. Start on a low speed and increase it gradually. If needed, use the tamper.

Good luck!

Buying and handling fruit and vegetables

Choose vegetables, fruit, and berries with care

The art of making delicious and healthy smoothie bowls begins at the fruit and vegetable counter—learning to find, choose, store, and use seasonal produce in the right way is the alpha and the omega. The crucial factor in finding the very best ingredients is using your eyes, nose, and hands, and, as far as possible, buying local.

Local markets and direct farm sales offer the freshest produce, usually at lower prices than regular stores. There are also several well-known companies that deliver fruit and vegetables directly to your door. They generally indicate the origin of their produce, the varieties they offer, and sometimes even the grower's references. Please see the Useful websites section at the back of the book for various companies operating home delivery of fruit and vegetables in your area.

Buy organic

Since many conventionally grown fruits and vegetables contain residues of fungicides, pesticides, wax, and spray, it's best to choose organic as far as possible. Besides, organic berries, fruit, and vegetables contain more vitamins, minerals, enzymes, and other nutrients than conventional ones, including higher levels of vitamin C and antioxidants.

Wash and scrub

Unless you pick fruit, berries, or vegetables from your own garden, there's no way of knowing how conventional produce has been treated, where it's been stored, or who has handled it—let alone whether it's been sprayed or waxed. Even fruits with inedible skin, such as bananas, oranges, mandarins, melons, mangoes, etc. should be properly washed, because everything that settles on your hands will pass into your body when you handle the flesh of the fruit.

If buying conventional produce, the simplest way to clean it is to fill a mixing bowl with lukewarm water, squeeze the juice of a lemon or a few tablespoons of vinegar essence in it, and immerse fruit, berries, vegetables, or lettuce in the solution for five minutes. The solution will release all the dirt without the fruit etc. taking on the flavor of the lemon or vinegar. You can use a soft vegetable brush to brush and then rinse off all hard-fleshed fruits and vegetables under cold running water. Never use the vegetable brush for any other purpose and make sure you carefully wash it after use. To wash soft-fleshed produce, rub it with your hands or with the soft side of a washing-up sponge. You should only use the sponge for washing produce. Lettuce, berries, and other sensitive produce should be rinsed under cold water after being pre-soaked in the lemon juice solution. An alternative is to buy special organic product washes.

To be on the safe side, make sure you also peel conventional fruit.

To peel or not to peel

Most vitamins, minerals, and enzymes are found just beneath or in the skin of fruit and vegetables. If you use organic produce, you should therefore, with a few exceptions, use the produce whole. Make sure you always peel citrus fruits (the zest has a bitter taste), all varieties of melon, banana, mango, papaya, kiwi, pineapple, and avocado. When peeling, always make sure you remove as thin a layer of the skin as possible.

Stones and seeds

The large stones of the avocado, apricot, mango, nectarine, peach, plum, and other stone fruits should be removed. It's best also to remove seeds, like those of melons and papaya, as they affect consistency. Please note, though, that you should refrain from eating papaya in large quantities if you are, or are planning to become, pregnant—in many countries of the world papaya is used as a natural contraceptive.

Freeze berries and fruit

The base of most smoothie bowls is made up of frozen fruits and berries. Not only do they ensure a thicker consistency, but they also provide natural sweetness and creaminess. Frozen banana, in particular, is the perfect base ingredient in a smoothie bowl as it's very difficult to achieve the creaminess that the banana provides using other ingredients.

I generally buy large quantities of organic berries and fruits in season, usually at local farmers' markets and farm sales. That way, I always have quality fruits in my freezer, even when they're not available in stores.

As mentioned above, the banana is the perfect fruit for freezing. Ensuring a fine consistency, it also provides natural sweetness. I buy large quantities of organic bananas, allow them to become almost over-ripe, then chop them into pieces, freeze the individual pieces, and then place them in plastic freezer bags. I always have 7–8 pounds / 3–4 kg of frozen banana at home, just to be on the safe side.

To freeze berries and smaller fruits, spread them out on a tray or a plate, covered with plastic wrap, and place in the freezer. To freeze larger fruits, peel and chop them into smaller pieces before freezing. When all the berries/pieces are thoroughly frozen, tip them into an airtight plastic bag, marking the contents, quantities, and dates for convenient use at a later date.

Tip! You can also freeze your own smoothie bowl mixtures containing berries and fruits that you think work well together. Then just tip them into the blender and blend with the remaining ingredients.

Serve immediately

To ensure you benefit fully from the flavor, consistency and, not least, the vitamins of your smoothie bowl, serve it as soon as possible after preparation.

Garnishes

Don't forget: it's fun, relaxing, and appetizing to eat really beautiful food. Serve smoothies in beautiful bowls or low glasses and garnish them with fresh or dried berries and fruits, nuts, seeds, herbs, edible flowers, and other fancy garnishes. I hope my images will inspire you to come up with your own garnishing ideas.

Nut, seed, and oat milks

Making your own nut milk is both easy and delicious. It's a healthy alternative to regular milk and an excellent substitute if you're lactose-intolerant or vegan.

Alternative milk can be made from various nuts and seeds, such as hemp seeds, cashews, hazelnuts, pumpkin seeds, pecans, pistachios, walnuts, sunflower seeds, or almonds. Go for unsalted, unroasted, and organic nuts and seeds: they taste the best, contain the most nutrients, and are free of pesticides and other harmful substances.

Soak the nuts and leave them in a cool place overnight in order to remove indigestible enzymes and to make the taste milder. Hazelnuts don't need presoaking, as they don't contain enzyme inhibitors. You can also blend coconut flakes and shelled hemp seeds without presoaking.

Strain off the water and rinse the nuts properly. Add more water and blend until the nuts are finely distributed in the liquid. Strain the milk through a nut-milk bag or fine sieve (shelled hemp seeds require no straining) and squeeze out as much of the liquid as possible. Flavor the milk with real vanilla, cinnamon, cardamom, or raw cacao and sweeten to taste with organic figs, apricots, medjool dates, coconut sugar, organic agave syrup, maple syrup, or honey.

Store the milk in a glass bottle or jar (it will keep longer than in a plastic bottle) for approx. 3–5 days in the refrigerator. Nut milks can also be frozen in ice-cube molds. You can use the remaining nut pulp to make nut balls, granola, muesli, and bread, or you can blend it into a porridge or smoothie bowl. The nut pulp freezes well, too, for later use.

I own a FoodSaver, a vacuum sealer that comes with a number of accessories, such as neat cans and bottle caps. It removes all the air from the container, which prolongs the nut milk's shelf life and preserves the flavor/appearance that little bit longer.

ALMOND, NUT, and SEED MILK
1 cup / 150 g soaked nuts, seeds, or almonds + 4 cups / 1 liter water + 1 pinch of Himalayan salt.

OAT MILK
1 cup / 90 g soaked organic rolled oats + 4 cups / 1 liter water + 1 pinch of Himalayan salt.

SESAME MILK
1 cup / 130 g soaked sesame seeds + 4 cups / 1 liter water + 1 pinch of Himalayan salt.

SOY MILK
1 cup / 175 g soaked soybeans or ¾ cup soy flour + 4 cups / 1 liter water + 1 pinch of Himalayan salt.

COCONUT MILK
1 cup / 90 g freshly grated or shredded raw coconut + 4 cups / 1 liter water + 1 pinch of Himalayan salt.

HEMPSEED MILK
¾ cup / 120 g shelled hemp seeds + 4 cups / 1 liter water + 1 pinch of Himalayan salt.

Protein powders

High-quality protein is extremely important for the body's constitution and functioning. It supplies the body with the building blocks it needs to create new, healthy, and strong cells, which in turn makes you less susceptible to disease and aging, reduces bad food cravings, and makes you feel fitter in general.

Most common protein powders are mixes containing different types of protein, but there are also protein powders made of a single source, e.g. hemp, pea, rice, pumpkin, and algae. For optimum balance I recommend that you switch between various protein powders.

There are many vegan variations on offer. It's important that the protein powder is organic and raw and free from bulking agents, trans fats, isolates, synthetic substances, artificial sweeteners, preservatives, or genetically modified (GMO) crops. The ingredients list should be as short as possible, so read it before you part with your money. The most common types of protein available, usually in health food stores, are:

HEMP PROTEIN: Extracted from shelled, ground hemp seeds; contains 50–55 percent high-quality protein. Often called nature's perfect protein as it contains all twenty amino acids, ten of which are essential, which is unique among vegetable proteins. It's also rich in nutritious dietary fiber and omega 3, 6, and 9 fatty acids. The flavor is mild and neutral. Don't confuse hemp protein with *hemp flour*, which consists of milled unshelled seeds containing a lot of shell residues.

PEA PROTEIN: Extracted from yellow peas; contains about 80 percent high-quality protein.

BROWN RICE PROTEIN: Extracted from sprouted brown rice; contains 80–85 percent high-quality protein.

OAT PROTEIN: Extracted from oats. In addition to around 50–55 percent high-quality protein, it also contains oat oil and oat maltodextrin, both of which occur naturally in oats. The flavor is mild and neutral.

SOY PROTEIN: Natural soy protein containing high-quality protein is extracted from soybeans; contains 60–70 percent high-quality protein. Soy protein has received a lot of criticism because it has often been treated with hexane, a powerful solvent similar to gasoline.

PUMPKIN PROTEIN: Rare, but is now beginning to show up on the market. Extracted from ground, shelled pumpkin seeds, it contains about 60 percent high-quality protein.

ALGAL PROTEIN: Spirulina and chlorella are the most common types, but protein is also extracted from arame, wakame, and dulse. They all contain many nutrients, vitamins, and minerals, and are up to 70 percent high-quality protein, depending on the type. The downside to algal protein is that it has quite a strong flavor and that it colors everything dark green.

Protein mixes or blends

Protein mixes usually contain several types of protein, e.g. that from brown rice, oats, peas, hemp, amaranth, quinoa, millet, buckwheat, garbanzo beans, lentils, adzuki beans, flaxseed, sunflower seeds, pumpkin seeds, chia seeds, or sesame seeds. Read the ingredients list carefully as undesirable ingredients are more common in a mix than in a powder made of a single source. Frequently, protein mixes contain stevia as a sweetener, but do make sure that you avoid artificial sweeteners.

Vitamins, minerals, and antioxidants

Vitamins

Vitamins are substances that are essential for life, but only in small quantities. The body cannot produce vitamins itself, so we have to obtain them by regularly eating a balanced diet. Humans need 13 different vitamins. They are divided into fat-soluble and water-soluble vitamins. Surplus fat-soluble vitamins are stored in body fat, while the water-soluble ones pass out with urine. It's difficult to feed your body some vitamins if you eat a vegan diet, so you may need to take supplements.

Fat-soluble vitamins

Vitamins A, D, E, and K are fat-soluble vitamins and are usually found in fatty foods, such as oils, milk, and fatty fish. The human liver contains large stores of fat-soluble vitamins; your store of vitamin D can keep you going for several months and that of vitamin A for up to two years.

Since fat-soluble vitamins do not mix so easily with water, any surplus cannot pass out with the urine. The body can therefore get too much of these vitamins (A and D) and be affected by poisoning symptoms. It's normally hard to ingest dangerous amounts of vitamins with your diet, but an overgenerous use of vitamin supplements may cause problems. People who wish to supplement their diets with vitamin tablets should therefore observe the recommended daily allowance (RDA).

VITAMIN A. Needed for eyesight and for the body's defense against infections. Carrots, among other fruits and vegetables, contain beta-carotene, which the body can convert to vitamin A.

VITAMIN D. Needed for strong bones. Your body can synthesize vitamin D itself if you get enough exposure to the sun. Vitamin D deficiency isn't usually down to a poor diet, but to a lack of exposure to the sun, perhaps because you're covering too much of your body or spending little time outdoors. Children under two get vitamin D drops.

VITAMIN E. Probably needed for the body's defense against free radicals.

VITAMIN K. Needed for blood to clot in case of a wound. Green leafy vegetables and cabbage, among other vegetables, are rich in vitamin K.

Water-soluble vitamins

The B vitamin family (B1, B2, B6, and B12), pantothenic acid (B5), niacin (B3), folic acid (B9), biotin (B7), and vitamin C are water-soluble vitamins. The eight B vitamins and vitamin C are found in many different foods. What they all have in common is that they easily disappear during cooking, because they leach out into the cooking water.

As a rule, water-soluble vitamins cannot be stored in the body. If you try to build up a store using vitamin tablets, the surplus will pass out with the urine. You should therefore replenish these vitamins regularly. Deficiency symptoms appear quickly if diet is inadequate. However, vitamin B12 is an exception: the liver builds a supply that will last you around four years.

VITAMIN B1 (THIAMIN). Is important for the body to convert energy from carbohydrates.

VITAMIN B2 (RIBOFLAVIN). Like vitamin B1, it's important for the body to convert energy from foods.

PANTOTHENIC ACID (VITAMIN B5). Needed for the body to use proteins, fats, and carbohydrates in metabolic processes. Sometimes, pantothenic acid is not considered a vitamin, because a lack doesn't cause any typical deficiency symptoms.

VITAMIN B6. Is a generic term for several substances needed for the body to break down and build protein.

VITAMIN B12. Needed, among other things, for cell metabolism, for blood-cell formation, and for the functioning of the nervous system. A substance produced in the mucous membranes of the stomach is needed for the body to absorb vitamin B12.

NIACIN (VITAMIN B3). Is important for the body to convert energy from foods.

FOLIC ACID (VITAMIN B9). Is important, among other things, for the body to produce amino acids and the building blocks of DNA. Pregnant women need additional folic acid so that the fetus can develop normally.

BIOTIN (VITAMIN B7). Needed for the body to produce and break down amino acids and fatty acids.

VITAMIN C (ASCORBIC ACID). Needed for the body to produce connective tissue and absorb iron from food. The body's immune system and its defenses against free radicals also depend on vitamin C. Vitamin C is also an antioxidant.

DESIGNATION	NAME	NEEDED FOR
Vitamin A	Retinol	Eyes, skin, mucous membranes
Vitamin B1	Thiamin	Metabolism, nerves
Vitamin B2	Riboflavin	Metabolism
Vitamin B3	Niacin	Metabolism, skin, nerves
Vitamin B5	Pantothenic acid	Metabolism
Vitamin B6	Pyridoxine, pyrdoxamine	Nerves, blood
Vitamin B12	Cobalamin	Blood, nerves, memory
Vitamin B9	Folic acid	Blood and memory
Vitamin B7	Biotin	Metabolism
Vitamin C	Ascorbic acid	Connective tissues, wound healing
Vitamin D	Cholecalciferol, ergocalciferol	Bones
Vitamin E	Alphatocopherol	Cell membranes, blood
Vitamin K	Phylloquinone, menaquinone	Blood clotting

Minerals

The human body needs about 20 different minerals. They are essential for life, but only in very small quantities. The mineral we need most of is calcium, which is found in the bones and teeth. Other minerals include phosphorus, potassium, sodium, and magnesium. Substances that we need only in very small quantities are called trace elements. They include iron, iodine, zinc, and selenium. If we eat a normal balanced diet, we'll usually ingest all minerals in sufficient amounts.

Antioxidants

Antioxidants are substances that protect us against oxygen radicals, i.e. harmful substances that form in our cells when they use oxygen to extract energy. Antioxidants that are particularly effective are vitamin C, vitamin E, beta-carotene, coenzyme Q10, and the metal selenium. By eating a diet rich in fruits and vegetables, you'll get the antioxidants that your body needs. There is no evidence that dietary supplements in antioxidant pill form are effective in preventing disease.

Blueberry, almond, and banana

Blueberries contain powerful antioxidants and are sometimes called superberries. They're good for the skin, eyesight, and night vision and they prevent glaucoma. Blueberries are also thought to be good for blood circulation in the legs and for fighting varicose veins, inflammation, blood clots, high blood pressure, and bad LDL cholesterol. The berries are also considered to be beneficial for diabetics because they regulate blood sugar. In addition, blueberries help with urinary tract infections and diarrhea.

Particularly beneficial are wild blueberries as they contain plenty of flavonoids, carotene, vitamin C, vitamin B6, and magnesium.

Serves one

7 tbsp / 100 ml almond milk

1 tbsp / 15 g almond butter

3 dates

1 tbsp vegan protein powder, vanilla flavor (optional)

1 tsp maca powder (optional)

1 pinch of cardamom, ground

1 banana, frozen

generous 1 cup / 150 g blueberries, frozen

Toppings
blueberries

coconut flakes, unsweetened

sprig of mint

1. Add the ingredients to the blender in the order listed and blend to a thick, frosty smoothie bowl.

2. Transfer to a bowl and top with the blueberries, coconut flakes, and fresh mint leaves.

3. Serve immediately and eat with a spoon.

Tip! Blend in a handful of fresh spinach for an even healthier version.

Zucchini and banana with spirulina

Spirulina is 60–70 percent protein, which is six times more than eggs and three times more than steak. Its protein consists of 18 different amino acids, 8 of which are essential. Spirulina also contains many essential minerals, including calcium, magnesium, sodium, potassium, phosphorus, iodine, selenium, iron, copper, and zinc; and a wide range of B vitamins, such as B1, B2, B5, B6, B11, and B12, as well as vitamins C and E. Its content of beta-carotene, which is converted into vitamin A in the body, is 15 times higher than that of carrots and 40–60 times higher than that of spinach.

Serves one

⅔ cup / 150 ml coconut milk

1 fig, dried or fresh

2 tbsp / 30 g cashew butter

2 tbsp chia seeds

¼–1 tsp spirulina powder (optional)

½ tsp cinnamon, ground

1 pinch sea salt (optional)

1 banana, frozen

1 zucchini, frozen

Toppings

granola of your choice

banana

raspberries

coconut flakes

goji berries

1. Add the ingredients to the blender in the order listed and blend to a thick, frosty smoothie bowl. Add some ice if you want a more ice-creamy consistency.

2. Transfer to a large bowl and top with granola, banana, raspberries, coconut flakes, and goji berries.

3. Serve immediately and eat with a spoon.

Tip! For an even healthier version, increase the spirulina powder up to 2 teaspoons. NB! Spirulina has a strong flavor, so go easy in the beginning until your taste buds get used to it.

Avocado, cacao, and açaí bowl

Avocados are chock-full of healthy fats that are thought to prevent wrinkles and improve brain capacity. Avocados have been considered an aphrodisiac through the ages. In addition to their possible potency-enhancing effect and beneficial monounsaturated fats, avocados also contain many nutrients that are good for the blood, liver, heart, skin, and hair. Avocados contain plenty of vitamin E, which makes the skin soft, supple, and healthy and gives hair extra shine. They're also high in potassium, which helps to regulate blood pressure and is good for muscles. The avocado also contains plenty of fiber, folic acid, and vitamins A, B, and C, as well as magnesium.

Serves one

7 tbsp / 100 ml almond milk

½ avocado

2 dates, pitted

2 tsp raw cacao

3 tsp açaí powder

1 banana, frozen

Toppings

banana

coconut flakes, unsweetened

raw cacao nibs or raw chocolate (90–100%)

1. Add the ingredients to the blender in the order listed and blend to a creamy smoothie bowl. Add some ice if you want a frostier consistency.

2. Transfer to a bowl and top with the banana slices, coconut flakes, cacao nibs, or chocolate crunch.

3. Serve immediately and eat with a spoon.

Summer berries & kale

Kale in a berry smoothie? I'm sure you're thinking I'm nuts, but this combination actually makes a delicious smoothie. You'll hardly taste the kale, so do give this smoothie bowl a try before you slash this recipe!

Kale is called 'The Queen of Greens' because it has the highest vitamin content of all the brassicas (broccoli, cauliflower, cabbage, red cabbage, and Brussels sprouts). Kale is rich in vitamins C, A, K, and B6 and also contains calcium, iron, copper, manganese, phosphorus, potassium, and several other minerals. Like all brassicas, kale promotes beneficial intestinal bacteria, purifies the blood, and detoxifies the body. Kale has also been reported to contain anticancer substances; it and other brassicas have been shown to limit cell growth in pancreatic cancer and reduce the risk of lung, gall bladder, urinary bladder, prostate, ovarian, and colon cancers.

The great thing about kale is that it's available from October to March, when many other locally and naturally grown vegetables are not.

Serves one

⅔ cup / 150 ml almond milk
2 tbsp / 30 g almond butter
1–2 tsp agave syrup or raw honey
4 leaves kale or a handful of baby spinach, chopped
1 tbsp bee pollen (optional)
1 tbsp chia seeds
1½ cups / 200 g mixed berries, frozen
1 banana, frozen

Toppings

strawberries

raspberries

blueberries

coconut flakes, unsweetened

bee pollen (optional)

1. Add the ingredients to the blender in the order listed and blend to a thick, frosty smoothie bowl. Add some ice for a more ice-creamy consistency.

2. Transfer to a bowl and top with the strawberries, raspberries, blueberries, coconut, and bee pollen.

3. Serve immediately and eat with a spoon.

Blackberry and coconut

A handful of blackberries contain almost half of your daily fiber requirement. Fiber keeps the intestines and digestion working. It also helps to regulate blood sugar in the body. Blackberries are also a good source vitamins C and E, potassium, manganese, magnesium, iron, and vitamin K, which help with the absorption of calcium, among other things.

Blackberries get their dark color from anthocyanin, a chemical pigment and antioxidative substance, which may reduce inflammation in the body and protect against free radicals that can otherwise damage cells and promote cancer.

Serves one

½ cup / 100 ml coconut milk

1 tbsp pumpkin seeds, unroasted

1 tbsp sunflower seeds, unroasted

2 tbsp coconut flakes, unsweetened

1 tbsp chia seeds

3 dates, pitted

1½ cups / 150 g blackberries, frozen

1 banana, frozen

Toppings
blackberries
pumpkin seeds
coconut flakes, unsweetened

1. Add the ingredients to the blender in the order listed and blend to a thick, frosty smoothie bowl. Add some ice for a more ice-creamy consistency.

2. Transfer to a bowl and top with the blackberries, pumpkin seeds, and coconut flakes.

3. Serve immediately and eat with a spoon.

Mint and chocolate

Raw cacao nibs are crushed cacao beans that have been roasted to 104°F / 40°C. This helps to retain almost all the nutrients, and no sugar is added. Cacao contains over three hundred nutritious substances, including high levels of antioxidants, magnesium, iron, chromium, and vitamin C. In addition, cacao contains endorphins, which produce feelings of pleasure and help to relieve depression.

There are studies showing that cacao increases nitric oxide levels in blood vessels, causing them to expand and blood pressure to drop. Low blood pressure in turn reduces the risk of stroke and heart attack.

Serves one

generous ¾ cup / 200 ml cashew milk

1–2 tsp agave syrup or raw honey

a few drops of mint oil, to taste

4 leaves kale, or small handful baby spinach, chopped

small handful mint leaves, fresh

2 tbsp raw cacao

2 tbsp raw cacao nibs

½ avocado

1 banana, frozen

Toppings

sprig of mint

raw cacao nibs or raw chocolate (90–100%)

flaked almonds

1. Add the ingredients to the blender in the order listed and blend to a thick, creamy smoothie bowl. Add some ice for a more ice-creamy consistency.

2. Transfer to a bowl and top with the mint, cacao nibs or chocolate crunch, and flaked almonds.

3. Serve immediately and eat with a spoon.

Strawberry dream

This tastes like strawberry mousse! How can something so rich in fiber be so creamy, tasty, and dessert-like?

Serves one

⅔ cup / 150 ml almond milk, unsweetened

1 tbsp / 15 g almond butter

½ tsp vanilla extract or vanilla powder

2 tbsp vegan protein powder (optional)

1 tbsp chia seeds

1 tbsp flaxseed

1 tbsp hemp seeds

1 tsp flaxseed oil

3 dates, pitted

1 banana, frozen

2 cups / 200 g strawberries, frozen

Toppings
strawberries
granola of your choice
coconut flakes, unsweetened

1. Add the ingredients to the blender in the order listed and blend to a thick, frosty smoothie bowl.

2. Transfer to a bowl and top with the fresh strawberries, granola, and coconut flakes.

3. Serve immediately and eat with a spoon.

Tip! Try adding a small handful of fresh baby spinach.

Coco-choco with chia seeds

Coconut oil is one of the world's healthiest oils. Although solid at room temperature, it becomes liquid at around 75°F / 24°C. Some 50 percent of the fat in coconut oil consists of lauric acid. The body converts lauric acid to monolauric acid, which is antiviral, antifungal, and antibacterial. Coconut oil contains the highest percentage of lauric acid of all the food products in the world. In addition, it's rich in caprylic acid, which promotes the growth of beneficial intestinal bacteria, fights fungi, and kills parasites in the intestinal tract.

Coconut oil is suitable for cooking, smoothies, and desserts, but it can also be used for body care. I use coconut oil instead of skin moisturizer. Always choose organic, raw, cold-pressed, unbleached, unrefined, and deodorized coconut oil. The ingredients list should state 100 percent coconut.

Serves one

4 leaves kale or small handful spinach

⅔ cup / 150 ml coconut milk

1 tbsp raw coconut oil

1 tbsp raw cacao

1 tbsp cacao nibs

1 tbsp chia seeds

2 tbsp vegan protein powder, vanilla flavor (optional)

3–4 dates, pitted

1 banana, frozen

ice (optional)

Toppings

chocolate granola, coconut flakes, unsweetened raw cacao nibs or raw chocolate (90–100%), coconut cream

1. Add the ingredients to the blender in the order listed and blend to a thick, frosty smoothie bowl. Add some ice for a more ice-creamy consistency.

2. Transfer to a bowl, top with chocolate granola, coconut flakes, cacao nibs, or chocolate crunch, and drizzle with a spoon of coconut cream.

3. Serve immediately and eat with a spoon.

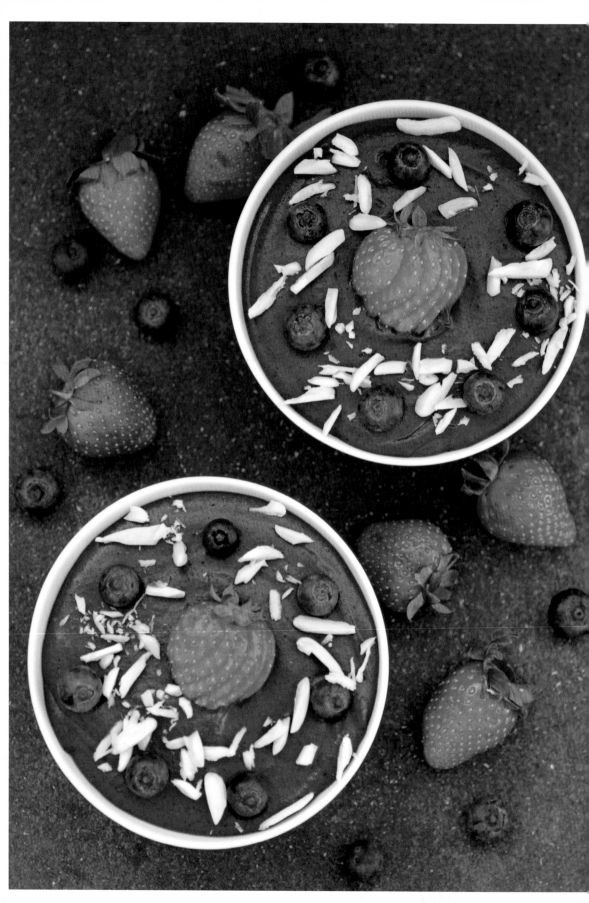

Açaí, kale, and berries

Açaí is a superberry native to South America's rainforests. It's packed with antioxidants, vitamins, and essential fatty acids and contains high levels of vitamin B, vitamin C, minerals, fiber, and protein. It also contains unusually high levels of potassium, calcium, iron, magnesium, copper, phosphorus, and zinc compared to other fruits and berries. Açaí is rich in anthocyanin, a beneficial antioxidant, which also gives the berry its purple color.

The açaí berry is actually a stone fruit. With only 10 percent of the berry being edible, the rest is stone. It has a dark and rich flavor—a fusion of blueberry, olive, and chocolate. In addition to its high vitamin and antioxidant content (seven times as high as that in blueberries) açaí also contains beneficial fatty acids.

Açaí has become a popular addition to smoothies and juices, but because the berries perish quickly, they're usually sold as pasteurized juice. However, much of the nutrient content is lost during the pasteurization process, so freeze-dried açaí powder is a better alternative on our side of the globe. The powder is available in well-stocked health food stores.

Serves one

4 leaves kale or handful spinach

generous ¾ cup / 200 ml almond milk, unsweetened

2 tsp hemp seeds

2 tsp açaí powder

¾ cup / 100 g blueberries, frozen

1 cup / 100 g strawberries, frozen

1 banana, frozen

Toppings
strawberries
blueberries
almonds

1. Give the kale and almond milk a quick blast in the blender.

2. Add the remaining ingredients in the order listed and blend to a thick, frosty, ice-creamy smoothie bowl.

3. Transfer to a bowl and top with the strawberries, blueberries, and almonds.

4. Serve immediately and eat with a spoon.

Cashews, hemp, and pineapple

Hemp seeds contain high levels of beneficial polyunsaturated fatty acids, omega 3, and omega 6. The seeds are as much as 25 percent protein and are rich in essential amino acids. They also contain high levels of calcium, magnesium, phosphorus, sulfur, carotene, iron, and zinc, and vitamins E, C, B1, B2, B3, and B6.

Hemp seeds are available in many different forms: shelled, unshelled, or as hemp protein powder, which makes an excellent natural protein supplement.

Serves one

small handful baby spinach

generous ¾ cup / 200 ml cashew milk

1 tbsp / 15 g cashew butter

2 tbsp hemp seeds

juice of ½ lime

¾ cup / 150 g pineapple, frozen

1 banana, frozen

Toppings
granola of your choice
cashew nuts, natural
hemp seeds

1. Give the spinach and cashew milk a quick blast in the blender.

2. Add the remaining ingredients in the order listed and blend to a creamy, ice-creamy smoothie bowl.

3. Transfer to a bowl and top with the granola, cashew nuts, and hemp seeds. Delicious, creamy, and good for you!

4. Serve immediately and eat with a spoon.

Wild strawberry and coconut bowl

Drinking coconut water has become quite popular, both as a restorer after a hard workout and as yet another addition to smoothies. Coconut water is the clear liquid found in young green coconut. Coconut water is 95 percent water, the remainder consisting of vitamins and minerals, such as vitamins B and C, phosphorus, calcium, and zinc. Coconut water is particularly rich in potassium and is sometimes called "nature's own sports drink."

Coconut water should not be confused with coconut milk, which is produced from the white flesh of a ripe brown coconut. Coconut water freezes well in ice-cube molds and keeps for six months in the freezer.

Serves one

7 tbsp / 100 ml coconut milk

7 tbsp / 100 ml coconut water

1 tsp coconut oil, raw

2 tsp chia seeds

2 tbsp vegan protein powder (optional)

2 tbsp coconut flakes, unsweetened

1 cup / 100 g wild strawberries, frozen

1 cup / 100 g strawberries, frozen

1 banana, frozen

Toppings

wild strawberries, coconut flakes, unsweetened pumpkin seeds, hemp seeds

1. Add the ingredients to the blender in the order listed and blend to a creamy, ice-creamy smoothie bowl.

2. Transfer to a bowl and top with the wild strawberries, coconut flakes, pumpkin seeds, and hemp seeds.

3. Serve immediately and eat with a spoon.

Tasty maqui, blueberry, and rolled oats bowl

The maqui berry is native to Patagonia in southern Chile. The berries rank high on the ORAC list, which compares antioxidant effects of foods. Maqui contains four times as many antioxidants as blueberries and twice as many as açaí. This makes maqui an effective weapon against free radicals. The berries also protect body cells against oxidative stress and fight premature aging. Antioxidants strengthen the immune system, suppress inflammation, and balance sugar levels. Maqui is also chock-full of flavonoids, , polyphenols, vitamins A, C, and E, and the minerals calcium, iron, and potassium.

Serves one

⅓ cup / 30 g rolled oats

⅔ cup / 150 ml almond milk

1 tbsp chia seeds

½ tsp vanilla extract

1 pinch of Himalayan salt

1 tsp bee pollen (optional)

1 tsp agave syrup or raw honey

1 tbsp vegan protein powder (optional)

2 tbsp maqui powder

1½ cups/ 200 g blueberries, frozen

1 banana, frozen

Toppings
blueberries
flaked almonds
bee pollen (optional)
sprig of mint

1. Mix the rolled oats, almond milk, chia seeds, vanilla extract, and salt in a bowl. Cover and leave in the refrigerator for at least 30 minutes or overnight.

2. Add the rolled oats mixture and the remaining ingredients to the blender, and blend to an ice-creamy smoothie bowl.

3. Transfer to a bowl and top with the blueberries, flaked almonds, bee pollen, and fresh mint leaves.

4. Serve immediately and eat with a spoon.

Piña colada bowl

Sweet, delicious pineapple contains a great deal of beneficial dietary fiber and vitamins to protect against viruses and infections. Above all, pineapple is rich in vitamin C, which builds connective tissue and helps the body to absorb iron from food. Vitamin C is also an antioxidant protecting against free radicals, which have a harmful effect on the body's cells. In addition to vitamins, pineapple is rich in bromelin, a very powerful enzyme when it comes to breaking down proteins, which in turn facilitates digestion. Bromelin is also good for blood circulation and it lowers blood pressure.

To find a good pineapple, look for one that looks plump. To check whether it's ripe, try gently pulling off a leaf. If it comes out, the pineapple is ripe. But it may also be overripe, so choose a pineapple the leaves of which don't come out easily, and allow it to ripen fully at home.

Serves one

7 tbsp / 100 ml coconut milk

1 tsp coconut oil, raw

2 tbsp coconut flakes, unsweetened

1 tbsp chia seeds

¾ cup / 150 g pineapple, frozen

1 banana, frozen

Toppings

pineapple pieces

fresh coconut, shaved

raw cacao nibs or raw chocolate (90–100%)

1. Add the ingredients to the blender in the order listed and blend to a creamy smoothie bowl. Add some ice if you want a frostier consistency.

2. Transfer to a bowl and top with the pineapple, coconut, and cacao nibs or chocolate crunch.

3. Serve immediately and eat with a spoon.

Cashew, mango, and strawberry

Cashews are naturally rich in iron, which both contributes to the formation of red blood cells and hemoglobin and reduces fatigue and exhaustion. Cashews are also rich in fiber and the minerals zinc, magnesium, and phosphorus.

The cashew nut grows on the Acajou tree. Encased in a hard shell, it grows on the tree's cashew apple, a fruit that looks like a sweet pepper, with a single nut attached to each apple. The nuts ripen when the apples fall from the tree. Then they're gathered and dried in the sun for a few days before being peeled and sorted.

Serves one

⅔ cup / 150 ml cashew milk

2 tbsp / 30 g cashew butter, raw

1 tbsp vegan protein powder (optional)

½ avocado

1 tbsp chia seeds

½ cup / 100 g mango, frozen

1 cup / 100 g strawberries, frozen

½ cup / 50 g raspberries, frozen

Toppings

mango

strawberries

cashews, natural

chia seeds

1. Add the ingredients to the blender in the order listed and blend to a creamy smoothie bowl.

2. Transfer to a bowl and top with the mango, strawberries, cashews, and chia seeds.

3. Serve immediately and eat with a spoon.

Raspberry, melon, and baobab

The baobab tree grows in the arid areas of Africa, Madagascar, and India.

The baobab fruit is sweet and sour, and rich in vitamin C, magnesium, iron, zinc, and calcium. It also contains substantial amounts of potassium and selenium.

Baobab powder is available in health food stores and online. Always buy organic raw baobab powder.

Serves one

⅔ cup / 150 ml almond milk

1 tbsp / 15 g almond butter, raw

1 tbsp baobab powder

2 tbsp vegan protein powder (optional)

1 tsp psyllium seeds

1 cup / 100 g raspberries, frozen

½ cup / 100 g melon, frozen in pieces

Toppings
raspberries
rolled oats
coconut flakes, unsweetened
pumpkin seeds
bee pollen (optional)

1. Add the ingredients to the blender in the order listed and blend to a creamy, frosty smoothie bowl. Add some ice if you want a more ice-creamy consistency.

2. Transfer to a bowl and top with the raspberries, rolled oats, coconut flakes, pumpkin seeds, and bee pollen.

3. Serve immediately and eat with a spoon.

Cherry, maca, and mulberry

Maca is extracted from the root of maca, which grows high up in the Andes, in Peru. Maca is known for its invigorating and energizing properties and has been used as a medicine in South America for centuries. The root was sacred to the Incas, and eaten before long journeys and battles in the belief that it improved strength and endurance.

The root is rich in vitamin C, potassium, calcium, iron, zinc, copper, manganese, and iodine.

Maca is said to relieve PMS and menopausal symptoms, such as mood swings and hot flashes. Maca is also said to be good for the skin and can help with acne and blemishes.

Serves one

⅔ cup / 150 ml almond milk

2 tbsp vegan protein powder

1 tbsp maca powder

1 tsp chia seeds

2 tbsp dried mulberries

½ tsp vanilla extract or vanilla powder

3 dates, pitted

generous 1 cup / 200 g cherries, frozen

1 banana, frozen

Toppings

cherries, mulberries, coconut flakes, sprig of mint

1. Add the ingredients to the blender in the order listed and blend to a creamy, ice-creamy smoothie bowl.

2. Transfer to a bowl and top with the cherries, mulberries, coconut flakes, and fresh mint leaves.

3. Serve immediately and eat with a spoon.

Mango, lúcuma, and spirulina

Lúcuma, an extremely hardy tree, grows in the Andes at altitudes of up to 7,875 feet. It can reach an age of 500 and continue to bear fruit. The lúcuma fruit is nutritious and tastes of toffee. Its soft sweetness makes it a healthy alternative to regular sugar. Not only is the fruit delicious, but it's also rich in fiber, antioxidants, vitamins, and minerals—especially vitamins C and B, beta-carotene, calcium, phosphorus, and iron. In lúcuma powder, all the nutrients are preserved in concentrated form.

The powder is available in well-stocked health food stores and is perfect for an extra boost of both flavor and goodness.

Serves one

⅔ cup / 150 ml almond milk

4 leaves kale or small handful spinach

1 tbsp vegan protein powder

½ avocado

2 tbsp lúcuma powder

½–1 tsp spirulina powder

¾ cup / 150 g mango, frozen

Toppings
kiwi

goji berries

strawberries

shelled hemp seeds

1. Add the ingredients to the blender in the order listed and blend to a creamy smoothie bowl. Dilute with more liquid if necessary. Add some ice if you want a frostier consistency.

2. Transfer to a bowl and top with the kiwi slices, goji berries, strawberries, and hemp seeds.

3. Serve immediately and eat with a spoon.

Banana, peanut, cacao, and goji berry

The goji berry has been discovered to be one of the most nutrition-dense foods on earth. The berry is unique because, among other nutrients, it contains 18 different amino acids, 7 of which are essential for life. In addition, goji berry is packed with essential minerals, such as iron, calcium, zinc, selenium, copper, calcium, phosphorus, and germanium. It's also rich in vitamins B1, B2, B6, and E.

Did you know that goji berries contain 500 times more vitamin C than oranges, three times more iron than spinach, and four times more antioxidants than cherries?

Goji berries can be eaten as they are, dried, or drunk as a juice.

Serves one

⅔ cup / 150 ml almond milk

3 tbsp / 45 g peanut butter, organic and without additives

2 tbsp vegan protein powder

2 tbsp raw cacao

2 dates, pitted

2 tbsp goji berries

1 tbsp hemp seeds, shelled

1 tbsp chia seeds

1 tsp flaxseed oil, cold pressed

2 bananas, frozen

Toppings

banana slices

coconut flakes, unsweetened

chopped peanuts, natural

raw cacao nibs or raw chocolate (90–100%)

1. Add the ingredients to the blender in the order listed and blend to a creamy smoothie bowl. Dilute with more liquid if necessary. Add some ice if you want a frostier consistency.

2. Transfer to a bowl and top with the banana, coconut flakes, chopped peanuts, and cacao nibs or chocolate crunch. This smoothie bowl tastes like a dessert!

3. Serve immediately and eat with a spoon.

Supergreen smoothie bowl

Spinach is a superfood high in antioxidants. The leaves are incredibly nutritious and contain, among other nutrients, vitamins A, C, E, and K, and vitamin B9 (folic acid). Spinach is also rich in copper, iron, magnesium, calcium, chlorophyll, fiber, and other beneficial substances.

Spinach contains high levels of an inorganic nitrate which is believed to increase the body's performance and muscle growth. Studies have shown that spinach makes the muscle cells' energy stations, the mitochondria, more efficient, which reduces the body's oxygen demand during physical exertion. Spinach is also considered to fight cancer and high blood pressure, and to be good for gastric ulcers.

Serves one

⅔ cup / 150 ml almond milk

1 tbsp / 15 g almond butter

¼ ripe avocado

1 handful spinach

3 leaves kale

1 tbsp flaxseed

1 banana, frozen

1 cup / 100 g strawberries, frozen

½ cup / 100 g pineapple, frozen

Toppings
granola of your choice, apricot slices, sunflower seeds, blueberries, chia seeds, goji berries

1. Add the ingredients to the blender in the order listed and blend to a creamy, ice-creamy smoothie bowl.

2. Transfer to a bowl and top with the granola, apricot slices, sunflower seeds, blueberries, chia seeds, and goji berries.

3. Serve immediately and eat with a spoon.

Apple crumble smoothie bowl

A new take on a classic... incredibly tasty and filling!

Serves one

⅔ cup / 170 g vegan vanilla yogurt

1 large apple, cored and chopped

1 tsp cinnamon, ground

½ tsp vanilla extract or vanilla powder

2 tsp coconut sugar

¼ cup / 40 g granola

3 dates, pitted

1 tsp chia seeds

1 banana, frozen

Toppings

dried apple slices

granola

dates

chia seeds

cinnamon

1. Add the ingredients to the blender in the order listed and blend to a creamy smoothie bowl. Add some ice for a frostier consistency.

2. Transfer to a bowl and top with the granola, dried apple slices, date slices, chia seeds, and cinnamon.

3. Serve immediately and eat with a spoon.

Hazelnut chocolate and hemp seeds

Hazelnuts are naturally rich in vitamin E, an antioxidant that protects cells against what is known as oxidative stress. The nuts are also rich in dietary fiber, magnesium, and the vitamin folate (folic acid).

Turkey is responsible for around 75 percent of the world's hazelnut production, but hazel trees and shrubs grow across virtually the entire globe, even in Sweden. After being gathered, the nuts are dried in the sun for 15–20 days.

Serves one

⅔ cup / 150 ml hazelnut milk

¼ cup / 30 g hazelnuts, soaked for at least 1 hour

2 tbsp hemp protein or 3 tbsp shelled hemp seeds

2 tbsp raw cacao powder

3 dates, pitted

1 tbsp chia seeds

2 bananas, frozen

Toppings

hazelnuts

dates

raw cacao nibs or raw chocolate (90–100%)

hemp seeds

1. Add the ingredients to the blender in the order listed and blend to a creamy, frosty smoothie bowl. Add some ice for a more ice-creamy consistency.

2. Transfer to a bowl and top with the hazelnuts, date slices, cacao nibs, or raw chocolate and hemp seeds.

3. Serve immediately and eat with a spoon.

Strawberry, mango, and chia seed bowl

Chia seeds are a real superfood: 3½ ounces / 100 g contain 1 ounce / 31 g fat, of which a full 0.7 oz / 20 g is linolenic acid, the vegetable form of omega 3. Two teaspoons of chia seeds contain more omega 3 than a normal-sized salmon fillet. Omega 3 is important for the body's hormonal balance and may have an anti-inflammatory effect. In addition, the seeds are rich in minerals, such as magnesium, potassium, and zinc.

In addition, 3½ ounces / 100 g chia seeds contain 0.74 ounces / 21 g protein, of which as many as 18 are amino acids. In other words, they're an important source of vegetable protein.

Chia seeds also contain copious amounts of water-soluble fiber, which promotes intestinal function and helps to keep blood-sugar levels even.

Serves one

7 tbsp / 110 g vegan vanilla yogurt
2 tbsp chia seeds
½–1 tsp ginger, freshly grated
1 tsp cinnamon, ground
½ tsp cardamom, ground
2 tbsp goji berries
2 dates, pitted
1 cup / 100 g strawberries, frozen
½ cup / 100 g mango, frozen
½ banana, frozen

Toppings
strawberries, mango slices, goji berries, sprig of mint

1. Add the ingredients to the blender in the order listed and blend to a creamy, frosty, and ice-creamy smoothie bowl.

2. Transfer to a bowl and top with the strawberries, mango slices, goji berries, and fresh mint leaves.

3. Serve immediately and eat with a spoon.

Peanut chocolate bowl

Peanut butter is really healthy. It's rich in fiber, protein, healthy fats, minerals, and vitamins. It also has a filling effect. A good peanut butter should be organically produced and consist of at least 99 percent peanuts. It shouldn't contain anything else, except perhaps a little sea salt. There are many different types available in retail stores, many of which contain both palm oil and sugar—watch out for them!

Serves one

7 tbsp / 100 ml water

4 tbsp / 60 g peanut butter

2 tbsp vegan protein powder

2 tbsp raw cacao

2 dates, pitted (optional)

2 bananas, frozen

Toppings

chocolate granola

banana

peanuts, natural

raw cacao nibs or raw chocolate (90–100%)

1. Add the ingredients to the blender in the order listed and blend to a creamy smoothie bowl. Add some ice if you want it to be frostier.

2. Transfer to a bowl and top with the chocolate granola, banana slices, whole and crushed peanuts, and cacao nibs or chocolate crunch.

3. Serve immediately and eat with a spoon.

Coconut and oat bowl

When coconuts ripen, the coconut water in them turns thick and milky—that's genuine coconut milk. The coconut milk that's available in cans in the supermarket is usually coconut extract mixed with water. Most cans give information about the coconut content and the amount of added water. Always buy unsweetened coconut milk without any additives.

Coconut milk is a creamy and delicious alternative to milk and cream in cooking, as well as being entirely lactose-free. The fat content may vary, but it's usually around 25 percent. Coconut milk is rich particularly in potassium, iron, magnesium, and phosphorus.

You can prepare small amounts of coconut milk yourself by blending grated coconut with water and then straining off the pulp. Coconut milk can be frozen in ice-cube molds.

Serves one

½ cup / 50 g rolled oats

¾ cup / 180 ml coconut milk

1 tbsp chia seeds

½ tsp vanilla extract

2–3 dates, pitted

1 pinch Himalayan salt

1 tbsp vegan protein powder (optional)

1 banana, frozen

Toppings

mango

raw cacao nibs or raw chocolate (90–100%)

coconut flakes, unsweetened

1. Mix the rolled oats, coconut milk, chia seeds, vanilla extract, dates, and salt in a bowl, cover, and leave in the refrigerator for at least 30 minutes or overnight.

2. Add the rolled oats mixture and the remaining ingredients to the blender and blend to a creamy smoothie bowl. Add some ice or one more frozen banana if you want a frostier consistency.

3. Transfer to a bowl and top with the mango slices, raw cacao nibs or raw chocolate, and coconut flakes.

4. Serve immediately and eat with a spoon.

Antioxidant smoothie bowl

Antioxidants are substances that protect us against free radicals, i.e. harmful substances formed in our cells when they use oxygen to extract energy. Particularly effective antioxidants include vitamin C, vitamin E, beta-carotene, coenzyme Q10, and the metal selenium. By eating a diet rich in fruit and vegetables, you'll supply your body with the antioxidants it needs.

Serves one

⅔ cup / 150 ml almond milk

1 tbsp pumpkin seeds

1 tbsp hemp seeds

1 tsp chia seeds

1 tbsp coconut flakes, natural

3 dates

⅓ cup / 50 g pomegranate seeds, fresh or frozen

¼ cup / 50 g cherries, frozen

½ cup / 50 g blackberries, frozen

½ cup / 50 g raspberries, frozen

1 banana, frozen

Toppings

muesli (see pages 103–104)

blueberries

raspberries

pomegranate seeds

coconut flakes, unsweetened

1. Add the ingredients to the blender in the order listed and blend to a thick, frosty smoothie bowl.

2. Transfer to a bowl and top with the muesli, blueberries, raspberries, pomegranate seeds, and coconut flakes.

3. Serve immediately and eat with a spoon.

Tip! Add a handful of fresh spinach for an even more antioxidant-rich version.

Tropical superfood bowl

A thick and creamy smoothie bowl with flavors of pineapple, coconut, and banana. The blue-green color comes from the super-healthful spirulina. You should use it sparingly until you get used to it, as it tends to overwhelm other flavors if you add too much. If the taste is too strong, you can tone it down by adding more ice, and making a frostier smoothie bowl.

Serves one

⅔ cup / 150 ml coconut water

1 tbsp / 15 g almond butter

2 tbsp coconut milk

1 tbsp baobab powder

½–1 tsp spirulina powder (optional)

½ apple, cored and cut into chunks

1 tbsp goji berries

2 tbsp / 30 g spinach, frozen

1 banana, frozen

½ cup / 100 g pineapple, frozen

¼ cup / 50 g mango, frozen

ice

Toppings
piña colada granola (see page 127), dried pineapple, coconut flakes, unsweetened, goji berries

1. Add the ingredients to the blender in the order listed and blend to a thick, frosty smoothie bowl. Add more ice for a frostier smoothie bowl.

2. Transfer to a bowl and top with the granola, dried pineapple, coconut flakes, and goji berries.

3. Serve immediately and eat with a spoon.

Superpower bowl

This is a really hardcore, supergreen smoothie bowl, filled to the brim with goodness and chlorophyll. On top of that, you get powerful antioxidants, such as turmeric, cinnamon, and cayenne pepper. The trick with a strong-tasting green smoothie bowl is to make it really frosty, so feel free to add more ice! Feeling tempted?

Serves one

⅔ cup / 150 ml coconut water

juice of half a lemon

3 tbsp / 25 g Brazil nuts, natural

¼ cup / 50 g kale, chopped

¼ cup / 50 g romaine lettuce, chopped

1 tbsp cilantro, chopped

1 tbsp parsley, chopped

3 figs, fresh

½ apple, cored and chopped into chunks

¼ cucumber, chopped

1 pinch cayenne pepper (optional)

1 pinch cinnamon, ground (optional)

1 tbsp fresh-grated turmeric
(or 1 tsp turmeric powder)

1 banana, frozen

ice (optional)

Toppings

raspberries

power muesli (see page 108)

Brazil nuts, chopped

coconut flakes, unsweetened

goji berries

1. Add the ingredients to the blender in the order listed and blend to a thick, frosty smoothie bowl.

2. Transfer to a bowl and top with the raspberries, muesli, Brazil nuts, coconut flakes, and goji berries.

3. Serve immediately and eat with a spoon.

Sea buckthorn, vanilla, and pineapple bowl

Sea buckthorn is a dioecious plant, meaning that there are distinct male and female plants. A single small sea buckthorn berry is said to contain as much vitamin C as a whole orange. However, the vitamin C content varies between 100 and 1,300 milligrams per 3½ ounces / 100 g of berries depending on the variety and ripeness. Sea buckthorn contains vitamin B12, which rarely occurs in plants and which is especially important for vegetarians. It also contains vitamins B1, B2, B3 (niacin), B6, B9 (folic acid), pantothenic acid, biotin, vitamin E, and vitamin K.

Serves one

7 tbsp / 110 g vegan vanilla soy yogurt
(or regular vegan vanilla yogurt)

2 tbsp vegan protein powder, vanilla flavor
(optional)

1 cup / 100 g sea buckthorn, frozen
(or 2 tsp sea buckthorn powder /
dried sea buckthorn)

4 figs, fresh

1 tbsp goji berries

2 tbsp coconut sugar

¾ cup / 150 g pineapple, frozen

ice

Toppings

granola (see pages 103–104)

sea buckthorn, fresh, dried, or frozen

figs, fresh

1. Add the ingredients to the blender in the order listed and blend to a thick, frosty smoothie bowl. Add more ice for a frostier consistency.

2. Transfer to a bowl and top with a granola or muesli of your choice, sea buckthorn, and figs.

3. Serve immediately and eat with a spoon.

Vanilla Nordic berry bowl

Classic Nordic berries include blueberries, (red, white, and black) currants, cranberries, sea buckthorn, gooseberries, raspberries, strawberries, blackberries, and cloudberries. They grow wild or are cultivated. The difference between wild and cultivated berries is that the wild ones contain far more vitamins, minerals, and antioxidants; they have a far more pronounced flavor, and they have a much more vibrant color. Cultivated American blueberries, for example, are totally different from blueberries growing in Swedish forests.

Serves one

7 tbsp / 110 g vegan vanilla soy yogurt (or regular vegan vanilla yogurt)

2 tbsp vegan protein powder, vanilla flavor (optional)

½ cup / 50 g blueberries, frozen (or 2 tsp blueberry powder)

½ cup / 50 g raspberries, frozen

½ cup / 50 g lingonberries, frozen (or 2 tsp lingonberry powder)

½ cup / 50 g blackcurrants, frozen

½ cup / 50 g sea buckthorn, frozen

3 dates, pitted

ice (if using berry powders)

Toppings
power muesli (see page 108), mixed berries, mint leaves

1. Add the ingredients to the blender in the order listed and blend to a thick, frosty smoothie bowl. Add more ice for a frostier consistency.

2. Transfer to a bowl and top with the power muesli, mixed berries, and mint leaves.

3. Serve immediately and eat with a spoon.

Plum and vanilla bowl

Plums are a perfect match for vanilla. The cinnamon in this recipe accentuates the flavors even more. I stone, quarter, and freeze any plums I don't eat in individual portions. Like that, they're ideal in a smoothie, in homemade jam, or in a yummy piece of pastry.

Serves one

7 tbsp / 110 g vegan vanilla soy yogurt (or regular vegan vanilla yogurt)

2 tbsp vegan protein powder, vanilla flavor (optional)

1 tbsp hemp seeds

1 tsp whole rosehip powder

1 pinch cinnamon

2 cups / 250 g plums, fresh or frozen

ice, if using fresh plums

Toppings

apple and cinnamon granola (see page 131)

plum slices

coconut flakes, unsweetened

1. Add the ingredients to the blender in the order listed and blend to a thick, frosty smoothie bowl. Add more ice for a frostier consistency.

2. Transfer to a bowl and top with the apple and cinnamon granola, plum slices, and coconut flakes.

3. Serve immediately and eat with a spoon.

Buckwheat and blueberry bowl

Buckwheat is actually a herb, but its beneficial properties and composition are similar to those of grains. That's why it's typically mentioned in connection with grains. Buckwheat is very easy to digest and is rich in thiamine, phosphorus, and magnesium. Since buckwheat is naturally gluten-free, it makes a perfect alternative to other types of grain or flour for the gluten-intolerant.

Serves one

7 tbsp / 110 g vegan vanilla soy yogurt (or regular vegan vanilla yogurt)

⅓ cup / 50 g buckwheat, soaked overnight

1 tbsp hemp seeds

1 tsp chia seeds

1 tbsp coconut flakes, natural

3 dates, pitted

1 cup / 100 g blueberries, frozen

1 banana, frozen

Toppings
blueberries, fresh or frozen
buckwheat, soaked overnight
coconut flakes, unsweetened
mint leaves

1. Add the ingredients to the blender in the order listed and blend to a thick, frosty smoothie bowl.

2. Transfer to a bowl and top with the blueberry, buckwheat, coconut, and mint leaves.

3. Serve immediately and eat with a spoon.

Almond and chia seed bowl with cinnamon

Cinnamon is produced from the bark of the cinnamon tree. The bark is peeled, dried, and rolled into cinnamon sticks, which are ground into a powder or sold as they are. Cinnamon contains the substance coumarin, which may cause liver damage if eaten in large quantities. Of the approximately 250 varieties of the cinnamon tree, Cassia cinnamon (*Cinnamomum cassiae*) and Ceylon cinnamon (*Cinnamomum verum*) are the most common. Ceylon cinnamon, which is sometimes called true cinnamon, is lighter, sweeter, and milder in flavor than cassia. Cassia is the type of cinnamon usually sold in Sweden. Cinnamon should be stored in a dark place in an airtight jar to preserve the aroma. I usually buy Sri Lankan Ceylon cinnamon sticks and grind them myself in a coffee grinder.

Serves one

7 tbsp / 100 ml almond milk

1 tbsp / 15 g almond butter

3 dates, pitted

1 tbsp vegan protein powder
(optional)

1 tbsp chia seeds

1 tsp cinnamon, ground

2 bananas, frozen

ice

Toppings

almonds, whole and chopped

chia seeds

dates, sliced

coconut flakes, unsweetened

mint leaves

1. Add the ingredients to the blender in the order listed and blend to a thick, frosty smoothie bowl.

2. Transfer to a bowl and top with the almonds, chia seeds, dates, coconut flakes, and fresh mint.

3. Serve immediately and eat with a spoon.

Carrot cake in a bowl

Carrots contain beta-carotene—a precursor of vitamin A. Vitamin A and carotene prevent cataracts and age-related changes in the retina, and are good for night vision. Vitamin A deficiency may cause night blindness. Carrots are also good for the skin. Carrots are best stored without their tops in a plastic bag in the refrigerator. You should cut off the tops because they sap the carrot's nutrients and cause it to soften.

Serves one

2 carrots, chopped

⅔ cup / 150 ml almond milk

2 dates, pitted

1 tbsp / 15 g almond butter, raw

1 tbsp hemp seeds

1 tsp cinnamon, ground

½ tsp ginger, ground; or 1 pinch freshly grated ginger

1 pinch nutmeg

1 tbsp maca powder

2 tbsp vegan protein powder (optional)

½ cup / 100 g pineapple, frozen

½ cup / 100 g peach, frozen

1 banana, frozen

Toppings

strawberries

homemade granola
(see pages 103–104)

goji berries

coconut flakes, unsweetened

bee pollen (optional)

1. Give the carrots and almond milk a quick blast in the blender.

2. Add the remaining ingredients in the order listed and blend to a creamy, ice-creamy smoothie bowl.

3. Transfer to a bowl and top with the strawberries, granola, goji berries, coconut flakes, and bee pollen.

4. Serve immediately and eat with a spoon.

Go-nuts-bowl!

Contains a variety of different nuts! If you don't have all the different nuts at home, just use those you have. To get the best out of nuts, I presoak them in a glass jar the night before. I then screw on the lid and leave them to stand in a cool place overnight – this allows the nuts to sprout. The indigestible enzymes disappear and the nuts become a "living food." The next morning, I rinse the nuts and blend them to a filling smoothie bowl.

Serves one

⅔ cup / 150 ml nut milk of your choice, or water
3 tbsp / 20 g hazelnuts, natural
3 tbsp / 20 g walnuts, natural
3 tbsp / 20 g cashews, natural
3 tbsp / 20 g pistachios, natural
3 tbsp / 20 g almonds, natural
1 tbsp hemp seeds
1 tbsp chia seeds
2 tbsp raw cacao
1 tbsp carob powder (optional)
3–4 dates, pitted
2 bananas, frozen
ice

Toppings
banana slices, muesli or granola of your choice
(see pages 103–104), mixed nuts, dates, sliced
hemp seeds, chia seeds, coconut flakes, unsweetened

1. Add the ingredients to the blender in the order listed and blend to a thick, frosty smoothie bowl.

2. Transfer to a bowl and top with the banana, muesli, nuts, dates, hemp seeds, chia seeds, and coconut flakes.

3. Serve immediately and eat with a spoon.

Blackberry and vanilla bowl

I've always been a sucker for vanilla. The scent alone is heavenly, not to mention the flavor.

Vanilla is sold in various forms. Pure vanilla powder consists only of ground vanilla beans. Vanilla extract is a liquid, and is made of vanilla beans infused in alcohol—easy to do yourself, but quite difficult to get hold of in Sweden. I always have vanilla beans at home, and I use them to make my own vanilla sugar. I almost never buy prepacked vanilla sugar. Vanilla sugar or essences often contain artificial flavorings.

Store-bought vanilla yogurt is usually too sweet for my taste, so I sometimes make my own vanilla yogurt. The easiest thing to do is to buy natural yogurt (animal or vegan) and stir in vanilla and a tiny bit of honey or agave syrup.

Serves one

7 tbsp / 110 g vegan vanilla soy yogurt (or regular vegan vanilla yogurt)

1 tbsp hemp seeds

1 tbsp coconut flakes, unsweetened

1 tbsp chia seeds

3 dates, pitted

2 cups / 200 g blackberries, frozen

Toppings
blackberries
coconut flakes, unsweetened
mint leaves

1. Add the ingredients to the blender in the order listed and blend to a thick, frosty smoothie bowl.

2. Transfer to a bowl and top with the blackberries, coconut, and mint leaves.

3. Serve immediately and eat with a spoon.

Almond, açaí, and vanilla bowl

The almond is commonly referred to as a nut, but in the botanical sense it's a stone fruit and is related to the plum, peach, and apricot, among other fruits. The actual almond grows like a seed inside the centre of the stone fruit. Almonds are 20 per cent protein. They also contain plenty of fiber and are particularly rich in vitamin E, iron, zinc, calcium, magnesium, potassium, and phosphorus, making them an ideal ingredient in a smoothie bowl after a hard workout at the gym.

Ready-made unsweetened almond milk is available in grocery stores, but you can make it yourself by blending almonds or almond butter with water. If you make it yourself, the milk will also contain more almonds than the store-bought variety. Please see page 21 for a recipe for homemade almond milk. Watch out for store-bought sweetened almond milk, as it contains a lot of sugar.

Serves one

⅔ cup / 150 ml almond milk

1 tbsp / 15 g almond butter

2 tbsp vegan protein powder, vanilla flavor (optional)

½ tsp vanilla powder or vanilla extract

3 tsp açaí powder

1 tbsp chia seeds

1 cup / 100 g strawberries, frozen

¾ cup / 100 g blueberries, frozen

1 banana, frozen

Toppings
blueberries, coconut flakes, unsweetened, sprig of mint

1. Add the ingredients to the blender in the order listed and blend to a thick, frosty smoothie bowl.

2. Transfer to a bowl and top with the blueberries, coconut flakes, and fresh mint leaves.

3. Serve immediately and eat with a spoon.

Rosehip, pineapple, and papaya bowl

Whole rosehip powder is easy to make yourself: just dry whole rosehips and grind them into powder. The powder contains 60 times more vitamin C than citrus fruits in addition to being rich in antioxidants and essential minerals, such as iron, calcium, potassium, and magnesium. Rosehip also contains folic acid, which is especially good for women who are breastfeeding or wish to become pregnant.

In the past, rosehip was used in popular medicine to prevent scurvy, i.e. vitamin C deficiency. Rosehip has also long been considered effective against constipation, fatigue, joint problems, diverticulosis, emphysema, ear problems, hemorrhoids, bladder discomfort, and colic, as well as stiffness in and problems with the back, legs, feet, and neck.

Serves one
⅔ cup / 150 ml water
¾ cup / 150 g pineapple, frozen
¾ cup / 150 g papaya, frozen
1 cup / 100 g strawberries, frozen
1 tbsp chia seeds
juice of ½ lime
2–3 tsp whole rosehip powder
2 tsp agave syrup or honey (optional)

Toppings
rosehip (if in season)
pineapple, cut into small pieces
papaya, cut into small pieces
seabuckthorn
chia seeds
coconut flakes, unsweetened
fresh mint leaves

1. Add the ingredients to the blender in the order listed and blend to a thick, frosty smoothie bowl.

2. Transfer to a bowl and top with the rosehip, pineapple, papaya, seabuckthorn, chia seeds, coconut flakes, and mint leaves.

3. Serve immediately and eat with a spoon.

Granola and muesli

There's something special about homemade granola. When you make it yourself, it sends an aroma of a fresh-baked cake through your kitchen. And as with cakes, you can create an infinite number of flavors—only your imagination sets the limits. The best thing about it is that you know exactly what you're eating: you won't have to consume huge amounts of sugar, which is common in store-bought granola, and you'll be able to increase the nutritional value by using a lot of nuts, seeds, and other goodness.

Granola can be baked in a conventional oven or dried in a dehydrator. I own an Excalibur. It consists of 9 ventilated trays (fitted with a mesh across) with a 15-foot / 1.4 m total drying surface area, as well as a timer with a 1–26-hour dial. It's quite expensive but well worth the investment if you're a raw foodie or want to make raw granola and natural sweets, or if you want to dry berries, fruits, vegetables, spices, mushrooms, and other tasty and nutritious goodies. I often use my dehydrator in the summer and fall so I can stock up for the winter.

The dehydrator's drying time very much depends on the indoor temperature and air humidity, as well as on how much moisture your ingredients contain. Your best bet is to taste the granola and touch it so you're sure you know when it's completely done. NB! It's important you follow the instructions for use specific to your own dehydrator.

Most of the granola recipes in this book can be made in both a conventional oven and a dehydrator. If baking granola in an oven, make sure you add nuts and seeds when the granola is out of the oven. That way, they'll retain most of the nutrients. The same is also true of dried fruits and berries because they burn easily.

If you're on a raw food diet, you shouldn't heat granola above 107–113°F / 42–45°C— that way you'll preserve all of its goodness. The downside to raw granola is that it doesn't become as crispy as granola baked in an oven; and that it has to be dried much longer, in some cases, even up to a day. Granola will turn out much crispier in a conventional oven and will develop a toasted surface and flavor.

I usually use a combination of a little melted coconut oil and date syrup, or agave syrup, maple syrup, or honey, in order to bind the ingredients, and make it a little sweet and crispy. I sometimes add dates that I've presoaked in hot water for a few hours, which I then blitz to a paste. Occasionally I'll also use a mashed ripe banana.

Unless you're a strict vegan or using a dehydrator, you can also stir in lightly whipped egg white for extra crispness before putting the granola in the oven. The egg white lends a crispness that is difficult to achieve without adding a lot of sugar. Whether or not you want to use egg white is entirely up to you—up to two egg whites will be about right for approximately scant 6 cups / 700 g of granola.

The difference between granola and muesli is that granola contains oil and sweeteners, and that it's baked, while muesli is fully raw, and doesn't contain any oil or liquid. Otherwise, the ingredients tend to be almost the same.

Making your own granola and muesli is dead easy. Granola takes a little longer to prepare and, if you're using a conventional oven, you'll need to watch it so it doesn't burn. In the following section I give some of my favorite granola and muesli recipes. Feel free to reduce/increase quantities or change ingredients if you feel like it.

Your muesli or granola will be what you put into it! All the ingredients should preferably be organic. The nuts, seeds, and grains should also be natural, i.e. unroasted, unsalted, and without additives. Coconut oil should be raw and organic. Dried fruit should preferably be sugar-free and oil-free. Raisins should definitely be organic, as they're among the fruits most treated with chemicals.

Presoaking

Nuts, seeds, quinoa, buckwheat, millet, amaranth, and other grains will be more healthful and easier to digest if you presoak or sprout them—this prior step ensures they start to germinate and become living food. If you do not have the time, energy, or inclination to soak or sprout the above foods, just use them as they are, i.e. *au naturel*.

Soak nuts, seeds, or grains in water in a jar, for at least 6–8 hours, or overnight. Make sure the water covers the ingredients completely. The day after, just rinse them a few times, and let them dry on paper or in a sieve. Do bear in mind, though, that granola takes longer to dry if it contains presoaked or sprouted nuts, seeds, or grains.

Storing

Make sure you store muesli or granola in a dry and dark place. That way, they'll stay crispy and fresh. For example, you can store them in a glass jar with an airtight lid, or in resealable or Ziploc® bags. I own a FoodSaver, a vacuum sealer that comes with a number of accessories, such as neat cans, plastic bags/plastic wrap, and bottle stoppers. It removes all the air from the container, which prolongs the granola's or muesli's shelf life. You can also use it to extend the shelf life of dried berries, fruits, vegetables, nuts, seeds, mushrooms, homemade smoothies, juices, and nut milk.

Homemade granola or muesli typically keeps for up to 1–2 months, but the longer it's stored, the tougher it will get. If it becomes tough, place it back in the oven, but on a slightly lower heat. Or redry it in a dehydrator.

Superseed muesli

MAKES ABOUT 4¼ CUPS / 500 G **PREPARATION TIME:** 10 MINUTES

This seed muesli is naturally gluten-free and extremely high in fiber. It's ideal for sprinkling over a smoothie bowl, porridge, or salad. Or why not add a few tablespoonfuls directly to a smoothie or smoothie bowl? The recipe makes about 4¼ cups of muesli, or 10–12 portions. You can replace the buckwheat with millet.

⅔ cup / 100 g buckwheat, natural

⅓ cup / 50 g hemp seeds, shelled

⅓ cup / 50 g chia seeds

⅓ cup / 50 g amaranth

¼ cup / 50 g quinoa, natural

⅓ cup / 50 g sunflower seeds, natural

6 tbsp / 50 g pumpkin seeds, natural

6 tbsp / 50 g sesame seeds, natural

3 tbsp / 30 g flaxseed, natural

4 tbsp / 30 g psyllium seeds

Mix all the ingredients in a large bowl.

Store in a dry, dark place in an airtight container at room temperature.

Power muesli

MAKES ABOUT 13 CUPS / 1.5 KG **PREPARATION TIME**: 10 MINUTES

I always have a supply of this divine fiber-rich and nutty muesli at home. A little goes a long way and will keep for a few months. The recipe makes about 3.3 pounds of muesli, but you can halve the ingredient quantities if you want to make a smaller batch. Feel free to exclude any of the ingredients you don't have at home or replace them with alternatives of your choice. It's ideal for taking into work in small, portion-sized, airtight resealable freezer bags.

4 cups / 400 g rolled oats (gluten-free, if necessary)

generous ½ cup / 100 g quinoa flakes

7 tbsp / 50 g hazelnuts, natural

⅓ cup / 50 g almonds, natural

7 tbsp / 50 g walnuts, natural

7 tbsp / 50 g pecans, natural

6 tbsp / 50 g pumpkin seeds, natural

⅓ cup / 50 g hemp seeds

⅓ cup / 50 g sunflower seeds

6 tbsp / 50 g mulberries, dried

generous ½ cup / 50 g coconut flakes, natural

6 tbsp / 50 g goji berries

6 tbsp / 50 g dried apricots, chopped

¾ cup / 100 g dried cherries, natural

¾ cup / 100 g blueberries, dried

¾ cup / 100 g cranberries, dried

¾ cup / 100 g raisins, seedless and organic

⅓ cup / 50 g chia seeds

⅓ cup / 50 g flaxseed

1 tbsp cinnamon, ground (optional)

1 tsp vanilla powder

1 pinch nutmeg, fresh-grated

1 pinch Himalayan salt or sea salt

Thoroughly mix all the ingredients in a large bowl.

This muesli is ideal for sprinkling over smoothie bowls, yogurt, sour milk, and almond or other nut milk.

Store in a dry, dark place in an airtight jar, or in resealable bags, at room temperature.

Tropical fruit muesli

MAKES ABOUT 6¼ CUPS / 800 G **PREPARATION TIME**: 10 MINUTES

I usually nibble on this muesli when I really can't beat my sugar cravings. It's also perfect sprinkled over a green smoothie bowl. During harvest season I usually dry fresh fruit to have on hand in the pantry all year round. When I buy dried fruits, they have to be organic and free of additives. The only additive I'll accept is ascorbic acid (vitamin C), which is sometimes used as an antioxidant agent in store-bought dried fruits. Some store-bought dried fruits may contain up to 50 per cent sugar and various vegetable oils, so watch out for them! A simple rule of thumb is that relatively heavy dried fruit usually contains a lot of sugar and oil.

3 cups / 300 g rolled oats
(gluten-free, if necessary)

⅓ cup / 50 g chia seeds

⅓ cup / 50 g hemp seeds

scant ½ cup / 50 g goji berries

generous 1 cup / 100 g shaved
coconut or coconut flakes

6 tbsp / 50 g pineapple, dried

6 tbsp / 50 g papaya, dried

6 tbsp / 50 g mango, dried

6 tbsp / 50 g banana, dried

3½ tbsp / 50 g coconut sugar

1 tsp vanilla powder

Thoroughly mix all the ingredients in a large bowl.

Good for sprinkling over smoothie bowls, yogurt, sour milk, or almond / other nut milk.

Store in a dry, dark place, in an airtight jar or resealable bags, at room temperature.

Fruit and nut mix

MAKES ABOUT 6¼ CUPS / 750 G **PREPARATION TIME**: 10 MINUTES

This is the ultimate on-the-go snack! I almost always carry this snack in my handbag, in my sports bag, or in the car—it's a life-saver when I don't have the time or opportunity to eat anything else. It gives me new vigor and energy, and silences the hunger pangs when I'm desperate for a bite. I portion the mix out in small airtight resealable plastic bags. An 11–15 ounce / 50–70 g portion will do.

The nuts should be natural, preferably organic and without additives. The raisins should definitely be organic, as they're among the fruits most treated with chemicals.

---

7 tbsp / 50 g pecans, natural

7 tbps / 50 g walnuts, natural

7 tbsp / 50 g Brazil nuts, natural

⅓ cup / 50 g almonds, natural

7 tbsp / 50 g hazelnuts, natural

7 tbsp / 50 g pistachios, natural

⅓ cup / 50 g sunflower seeds, natural

6 tbsp / 50 g pumpkin seeds, natural

¾ cup / 100 g raisins, seedless

6 tbsp / 50 g physalis, dried

6 tbsp / 50 g cranberries, dried

6 tbsp / 50 g banana, dried

6 tbsp / 50 g mulberries, dried

6 tbsp / 50 g goji berries, dried

Thoroughly mix all the ingredients in a large bowl.

Good for sprinkling over a smoothie bowl, yoghurt, sour milk, or morning porridge.

Store in a dry, dark place, in an airtight jar or resealable plastic bags, at room temperature.

Millet granola with nuts and cinnamon

MAKES ABOUT SCANT 6 CUPS / 750 G **PREPARATION TIME:** 10 MINUTES
BAKING TIME IN THE OVEN: 40–50 MINUTES **IN THE DEHYDRATOR:** 8–12 HOURS

Dry ingredients

1½ cups / 150 g rolled oats (gluten-free, if necessary)

¾ cup / 150 g millet, natural

generous ¾ cup / 100 g walnuts, chopped

generous ¾ cup / 100 g pecans, chopped

⅓ cup / 50 g flaxseed

3 tsp cinnamon, ground

1 pinch nutmeg, fresh-grated

1 pinch cardamom, ground

1 pinch Himalayan salt or sea salt

¾ cup / 100 g raisins, seedless and organic

dried banana slices

Wet ingredients

1 banana, ripe

2 tbsp coconut oil, raw

4 tbsp maple syrup

4 tbsp tahini

1 tsp vanilla extract

1 egg white, lightly whipped (optional)

Method

1. Mash the banana with a fork.

2. Mix all the wet ingredients until smooth in a bowl. Omit the egg white if you're on a strict vegan diet or using a dehydrator. Add more maple syrup if you want a sweeter-tasting granola.

3. In another large-sized bowl, mix all the dry ingredients except for the raisins and dried banana slices. They need to be stirred in after the baking.

4. Combine the wet and dry ingredients and stir well to finish the mixture. ➔

5. OVEN METHOD

» Preheat the oven to 300°F / 150°C.

» Cover one or two cookie sheets with parchment paper.

» Spread the mixture over the paper in an even layer.

» Bake the granola until it turns golden brown, 40–50 minutes, making sure to stir thoroughly halfway through the baking time (the less you stir, the chunkier the granola will be). Keep a close eye on the granola so it doesn't burn. It should be crispy and dry, and get some color.

» Turn off the oven, open the oven door slightly, and allow to dry in the residual heat.

DEHYDRATOR METHOD

» Cover several trays with greaseproof paper.

» Spread the mixture evenly over the trays.

» Dry at 107–113°F / 42–45°C for 6–8 hours.

» Take the granola out, remove the greaseproof paper, and spread the granola over the tray (same as before, but without the greaseproof paper).

» Dry for another 2–4 hours. The granola should be completely dry. The drying time very much depends on the indoor temperature and air humidity, as well as on its moisture content. Taste and touch the granola so you're sure it's completely done. NB! Follow the dehydrator instructions.

6. Allow the granola to cool completely and stir in the raisins and dried banana slices. It should turn even crispier once cool.

7. Store in a dry, dark place, in an airtight jar. The granola will keep for several months, but the longer it's stored, the tougher it will get.

Crispy coconut and quinoa granola with chocolate

MAKES ABOUT 6¼ CUPS / 800 G **PREPARATION TIME:** 10 MINUTES **BAKING TIME IN THE OVEN:** 40–50 MINUTES **IN THE DEHYDRATOR:** 8–12 HOURS

Dry ingredients

1½ cup / 150 g rolled oats (gluten-free, if necessary)

1 cup / 150 g quinoa, natural

1 cup / 150 g almonds, natural

⅓ cup / 50 g chia seeds

1 tsp cinnamon, ground

2–4 tbsp cacao, raw (to taste)

2 tbsp carob powder (optional)

1 pinch Himalayan salt or sea salt

1 ⅔ cups / 150 g shaved or grated coconut, natural

¾ cup / 100 g raisins, seedless and organic

5 tbsp / 50 g cacao nibs or raw chocolate, 70–85% raw chocolate, chopped (optional)

Wet ingredients

4 tbsp agave syrup or raw honey

3 tbsp coconut oil, melted

1 tsp vanilla extract

1 egg white, lightly beaten (optional)

Method

1. Mix all the wet ingredients, except the egg white, in a saucepan and heat over a low heat until the mixture becomes a little more fluid. Stir thoroughly until smooth. NB! Don't heat the mixture above 113°F / 45°C, i.e. a little warmer than warm to the touch. Add more agave syrup or honey for a sweeter-tasting granola. If desired, stir in the egg white for a crispier granola. Omit the egg white if you're on a strict vegan diet or using a dehydrator. ➔

2. Mix together the rolled oats, quinoa, almonds, chia seeds, cinnamon, cacao, carob powder, and salt in a large bowl. NB! If using the oven, add the coconut when the granola is almost done. If using the dehydrator, stir it in now. Stir in the raisins and cacao nibs/raw chocolate when the granola is done and has cooled.

3. Combine the wet and dry ingredients.

4. OVEN METHOD

» Preheat the oven to 300°F / 150°C.

» Cover one or two cookie sheets with parchment paper.

» Spread the mixture over the paper evenly.

» Bake the granola for 40–50 minutes, making sure to stir carefully halfway through the baking time (the less you stir, the chunkier the granola will be).

» Sprinkle over the coconut when the granola is almost done (coconut burns easily and should only be toasted for a few minutes). Keep a close eye on the granola so it doesn't burn. It should be crispy and dry. It's hard to see when dark granola is done, so go by smell and taste.

» Turn off the oven, open the oven door slightly and allow to dry in the residual heat.

DEHYDRATOR METHOD

» Cover several trays with greaseproof paper.

» Spread the mixture to form a thin layer.

» Dry at 107–113°F / 42–45°C for 6–8 hours.

» Take the granola out, remove the greaseproof paper, and spread the granola over the tray (same as before, but without the greaseproof paper).

» Dry for another 2–4 hours. The granola should be completely dry. The drying time very much depends on the indoor temperature and air humidity, as well as on its moisture content. Taste and touch the granola so you're sure it's completely done. NB! Follow the dehydrator instructions.

5. When the granola is done, allow it to cool and then stir in the raisins and chopped chocolate. It should turn even crispier once cool.

6. Store in a dry, dark place, in an airtight jar. The granola will keep for several months, but the longer it's stored, the tougher it will get.

Buckwheat granola with chocolate, figs, and dates

MAKES ABOUT 6 CUPS / 850 G **PREPARATION TIME:** 10 MINUTES
BAKING TIME IN THE OVEN: 40–50 MINUTES **IN THE DEHYDRATOR:** 8–12 HOURS

Dry ingredients

1½ cups / 150 g rolled oats (gluten-free, if necessary)

1 cup / 150 g buckwheat, natural

generous ¾ cup / 100 g hazelnuts, natural, chopped

½ cup / 50 g cashews, natural, chopped

½ cup / 50 g almonds, natural, chopped

⅓ cup / 50 g chia seeds

2–4 tbsp cacao, raw (to taste)

1 pinch Himalayan salt or sea salt

¾ cup / 100 g dried dates, stoned and chopped

scant ½ cup / 50 g dried figs, chopped

generous ¾ cup / 100 g cacao nibs or raw chocolate, 70–85% raw chocolate, chopped (optional)

Wet ingredients

4 tbsp date syrup or raw honey

3 tbsp coconut oil, melted

1 tsp vanilla extract (optional)

1 egg white, lightly beaten (optional)

Method

1. Mix all the wet ingredients, except the egg white, in a saucepan and heat over a low heat until the mixture becomes a little more fluid. Stir thoroughly until smooth. NB! Don't heat the mixture above 113°F / 45°C, i.e. a little warmer than warm to the touch. Add more date syrup or honey for a sweeter-tasting granola. If desired, stir in the egg white for a crispier granola. Omit the egg white if you're on a strict vegan diet or using a dehydrator. ➜

2. Mix together the rolled oats, buckwheat, hazelnuts, cashews, almonds, chia seeds, cacao, and salt in a large bowl. NB! Stir in the dates, figs, and cacao nibs/raw chocolate when the granola is done and has cooled.

3. Combine the wet and dry ingredients.

4. OVEN METHOD

» Preheat the oven to 300°F / 150°C.

» Cover one or two cookie sheets with parchment paper.

» Spread the mixture over the paper evenly.

» Bake the granola for 40–50 minutes, making sure to stir carefully halfway through the baking time (the less you stir, the chunkier the granola will be). Keep a close eye on the granola so it doesn't burn. It's hard to see when dark granola is done, so go by smell and taste.

» Turn off the oven, open the oven door slightly and allow to dry in the residual heat.

DEHYDRATOR METHOD

» Cover several trays with greaseproof paper.

» Spread the mixture to form a thin layer.

» Dry at 107–113°F / 42–45°C for 6–8 hours.

» Take the granola out, remove the greaseproof paper, and spread the granola over the trays (same as before, but without the greaseproof paper).

» Dry for another 2–4 hours. The granola should be completely dry. The drying time very much depends on the indoor temperature and air humidity, as well as on its moisture content. Taste and touch the granola so you're sure it's completely done. NB! Follow the dehydrator instructions.

5. When the granola is done, allow it cool completely and then stir in the dates, figs, and cacao nibs or raw chocolate. It should turn even crispier once cool.

6. Store in a dry, dark place, in an airtight jar. The granola will keep for several months, but the longer it's stored, the tougher it will get.

Piña colada granola with amaranth

MAKES ABOUT 6 ⅔ CUPS / 750 G **PREPARATION TIME:** 10 MINUTES
BAKING TIME IN THE OVEN: 40–50 MINUTES **IN THE DEHYDRATOR:** 8–12 HOURS

Dry ingredients

2 cups / 200 g rolled oats (gluten-free, if necessary)

scant ½ cup / 100 g amaranth, natural

½ cup / 50 g almonds, natural, chopped

½ cup / 50 g cashews, natural, chopped

⅓ cup / 50 g chia seeds

1 pinch Himalayan salt or sea salt

1 ⅔ cups / 150 g shaved or grated coconut, natural

¾ cup / 100 g dried pineapple, preferably unsweetened, chopped

Wet ingredients

4–5 tbsp agave syrup or raw honey

4 tbsp coconut oil, melted

1 tsp vanilla extract (optional)

1–2 egg white(s), lightly beaten (optional)

Method

1. Mix all the wet ingredients, except the egg white(s), in a saucepan and heat over a low heat until the mixture becomes a little more fluid. Stir thoroughly until smooth. NB! Don't heat the mixture above 113°F / 45°C, i.e. a little warmer than warm to the touch. Add more agave syrup or honey for a sweeter-tasting granola. If desired, stir in the egg white for a crispier granola. Omit the egg white if you're on a strict vegan diet or using a dehydrator.

2. Stir together the rolled oats, amaranth, almonds, cashews, chia seeds, and salt in a large bowl. NB! If using the oven, add the coconut when the granola is almost done. If using the dehydrator, stir it in now. Otherwise, stir it in when the granola is done and has cooled. →

3. Combine the wet and dry ingredients.

4. OVEN METHOD

» Preheat the oven to 300°F / 150°C.

» Cover one or two cookie sheets with parchment paper.

» Spread the mixture over the paper evenly.

» Bake the granola for 40–50 minutes, making sure to stir carefully halfway through the baking time (the less you stir, the chunkier the granola will be).

» Sprinkle over the coconut when the granola is almost done (coconut burns easily and should only be toasted for a few minutes). Keep a close eye on the granola so it doesn't burn. It should be crispy and dry, and have acquired some color.

» Turn off the oven, open the oven door slightly and allow to dry in the residual heat.

DEHYDRATOR METHOD

» Cover several trays with greaseproof paper.

» Spread the mixture to form a thin layer.

» Dry at 107–113°F / 42–45°C for 6–8 hours.

» Take the granola out, remove the greaseproof paper, and spread the granola over the trays (same as before, but without the greaseproof paper).

» Dry for another 2–4 hours. The granola should be completely dry. The drying time very much depends on the indoor temperature and air humidity, as well as on its moisture content. Taste and touch the granola so you're sure it's completely done. NB! Follow the dehydrator instructions.

5. When the granola is done, allow it cool completely, and then stir in the pineapple. It should turn even crispier once cool.

6. Store in a dry, dark place, in an airtight jar. The granola will keep for several months, but the longer it's stored, the tougher it will get.

Cinnamon and apple granola

MAKES ABOUT 6 ⅔ CUPS / 850 G **PREPARATION TIME:** 10 MINUTES
BAKING TIME IN THE OVEN: 40–50 MINUTES **IN THE DEHYDRATOR:** 8–12 HOURS

Dry ingredients

3 cups / 200 g rolled oats (gluten-free, if necessary)

scant ½ cup / 100 g quinoa or millet, natural

generous ¾ cup / 100 g almonds, natural, chopped

⅔ cup / 100 g pumpkin seeds, natural

⅓ cup / 50 g flaxseed

4 tsp cinnamon, ground

½ tsp nutmeg, fresh-grated

½–1 tsp ginger, ground

¼ tsp cloves, ground

1 pinch Himalayan salt or sea salt

¾ cup / 100 g dried apples, preferably unsweetened

¾ cup / 100 g raisins, seedless and organic

Wet ingredients

5 tbsp apple sauce

4–5 tbsp agave syrup or raw honey

4 tbsp coconut oil, melted

1 tsp vanilla extract (optional)

1–2 egg whites, lightly beaten (optional)

Method

1. Mix all the wet ingredients, except the egg white(s), in a saucepan and heat over a low heat until the mixture becomes a little more fluid. Stir thoroughly until smooth. NB! Don't heat the mixture above 113°F / 45°C, i.e. a little warmer than warm to the touch. Add more agave syrup or honey for a sweeter-tasting granola. If desired, stir in the egg white(s) for a crispier granola. Omit the egg white(s) if you're on a strict vegan diet or using a dehydrator. →

2. Mix together the rolled oats, quinoa, almonds, pumpkin seeds, flax seeds, and salt in a large bowl. NB! Stir in the apples and raisins when the granola is done and has cooled.

3. Combine the wet and dry ingredients.

4. OVEN METHOD

» Preheat the oven to 300°F / 150°C.

» Cover one or two cookie sheets with parchment paper.

» Spread the mixture over the paper evenly.

» Bake the granola for 40–50 minutes, making sure to stir carefully halfway through the baking time (the less you stir, the chunkier the granola will be).

» Keep a close eye on the granola so it doesn't burn. It should be crispy and dry, and have acquired some color.

» Turn off the oven, open the oven door slightly and allow to dry in the residual heat.

DEHYDRATOR METHOD

» Cover several trays with greaseproof paper.

» Spread the mixture to form a thin layer.

» Dry at 107–113°F / 42–45°C for 6–8 hours.

» Take the granola out, remove the greaseproof paper, and spread the granola over the trays (same as before, but without the greaseproof paper).

» Dry for another 2–4 hours. The granola should be completely dry. The drying time very much depends on the indoor temperature and air humidity, as well as on its moisture content. Taste and touch the granola so you're sure it's completely done. NB! Follow the dehydrator instructions.

5. When the granola is done, allow it to cool completely, and then stir in the dried apples and raisins. It should turn even crispier once cool.

6. Store in a dry, dark place, in an airtight jar. The granola will keep for several months, but the longer it's stored, the tougher it will get.

Blueberry, raspberry, and strawberry granola

MAKES ABOUT 6¼ CUPS / 750 G **PREPARATION TIME:** 10 MINUTES
BAKING TIME IN THE OVEN: 40–50 MINUTES **IN THE DEHYDRATOR:** 8–12 HOURS

The sweetened blueberries make this granola a luxurious treat. If you prefer, feel free to use unsweetened ones. The tart strawberries and raspberries lift the flavor.

Dry ingredients

2½ cups / 250 g rolled oats (gluten-free, if necessary)

generous ½ cup / 100 g quinoa, natural

⅓ cup / 50 g chia seeds

1 pinch Himalayan salt or sea salt

generous 1 cup / 100 g grated coconut, natural

¾ cup / 100 g dried blueberries, sweetened

6 tbsp / 50 g dried raspberries, natural

6 tbsp / 50 g dried strawberries, natural

Wet ingredients

4–5 tbsp agave syrup or raw honey

4 tbsp coconut oil, melted

2 tsp vanilla extract (optional)

1–2 egg white(s), lightly beaten (optional)

Method

1. Mix all the wet ingredients, except the egg white(s), in a saucepan and heat over a low heat until the mixture becomes a little more fluid. Stir thoroughly until smooth. NB! Don't heat the mixture above 113°F / 45°C, i.e. a little warmer than warm to the touch. Add more agave syrup or honey for a sweeter-tasting granola. If desired, stir in the egg white(s) for a crispier granola. Omit the egg white(s) if you're on a strict vegan diet or using a dehydrator. ➔

2. Mix together the rolled oats, quinoa, chia seeds, and salt in a large bowl. NB! If using the oven, add the coconut when the granola is almost done. If using the dehydrator, stir it in now. When the granola is done and has cooled, stir in the blueberries, raspberries, and strawberries.

3. Combine the wet and dry ingredients.

4. OVEN METHOD

» Preheat the oven to 300°F / 150°C.

» Cover one or two cookie sheets with parchment paper.

» Spread the mixture over the paper evenly.

» Bake the granola for 40–50 minutes, making sure to stir carefully halfway through the baking time (the less you stir, the chunkier the granola will be).

» Sprinkle over the coconut when the granola is almost done (coconut burns easily and should only be toasted for a few minutes). Keep a close eye on the granola so it doesn't burn. It should be crispy and dry, and get some color.

» Turn off the oven, open the oven door slightly and allow to dry in the residual heat.

DEHYDRATOR METHOD

» Cover several trays with greaseproof paper.

» Spread the mixture to form a thin layer.

» Dry at 107–113°F / 42–45°C for 6–8 hours.

» Take the granola out, remove the greaseproof paper, and spread the granola over the trays (same as before, but without the greaseproof paper).

» Dry for another 2–4 hours. The granola should be completely dry. The drying time very much depends on the indoor temperature and air humidity, as well as on its moisture content. Taste and touch the granola so you're sure it's completely done. NB! Follow the dehydrator instructions.

5. When the granola is done, allow it to cool completely, and then stir in the blueberries, raspberries, and strawberries. It should turn even crispier once cool.

6. Store in a dry, dark place, in an airtight jar. The granola will keep for several months, but the longer it's stored, the tougher it will get.

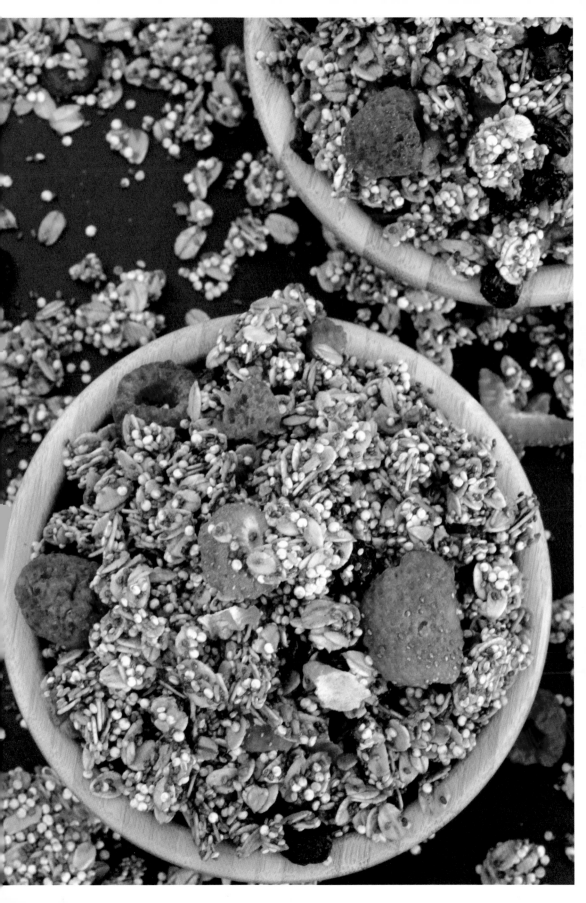

Useful websites

http://nutritionfacts.org/

http://www.davidwolfe.com/

http://www.fullyraw.com/

http://youngonrawfood.com/

http://www.juicemaster.com/

Acknowledgements

... my beloved daughter **Jasmine** for brightening up every day of my life.

... my beloved husband and agent, **Stefan Lindström**, for tasting all the recipes I dream up, and for taking such lovely photos of me. This book wouldn't have been possible without you.

... **Birgitta Torstendahl** at Akademibokhandeln for planting the seed for this book.

... my dear brother, **Alan Maranik**, for giving this book an incredibly attractive design. It's always fun working with you.

... my editor, **Eva Stjerne**, for the great linguistic backup – as always.

... **Christer Lindblom** at Stevali for helping me to get the book out into bookstores throughout Sweden.

... **Carl Uggla** at Lindenbaum Agenturer for all your valuable advice, the Vitamix blenders, and Omega juicers. What brilliant powerhouses they are!

... **Lars Malmqvist** at Linderholm for the vacuum sealer and accessories from FoodSaver. It helps to keep my granolas, muesli, juices, smoothies, and fruits fresher for longer.

... Herbert Ullmann, Florian Ullmann, Pierre Toromanoff, Lars Pietzschmann, Isabel Weiler, Katharina Pferdmenges and everyone at Ullmann Publishing and Tandem Verlag, who are working to publish my books across the globe.

Recipe index

Smoothie bowls

Granola and muesli

Abbreviations and Quantities

1 oz = 1 ounce = 28 grams
1 lb = 1 pound = 16 ounces 1
1 cup = approx. 5–8 ounces* (see below)
1 cup = 8 fl uid ounces = 250 milliliters (liquids)
2 cups = 1 pint (liquids) = 15 milliliters (liquids)
8 pints = 4 quarts = 1 gallon (liquids)
1 g = 1 gram = 1/1000 kilogram = 5 ml (liquids)
1 kg = 1 kilogram = 1000 grams = 2¼ lb
l l = 1 liter = 1000 milliliters (ml) = 1 quart
125 milliliters (ml) = approx. 8 tablespoons = ½ cup
1 tbsp = 1 level tablespoon = 15–20 g* (depending on
density) = 15 milliliters (liquids)
1 tsp = 1 level teaspoon = 3–5 g * (depending on
density) = 5 ml (liquids)

*The weight of dry ingredients varies significantly
depending on the density factor, e.g. 1 cup of
flour weighs less than 1 cup of butter. Quantities
in ingredients have been rounded up or down for
convenience, where appropriate. Metric conversions
may therefore not correspond exactly. It is important
to use either American or metric measurements
within a recipe.

© Eliq Maranik and Stevali Production
Original title: *Smoothie bowls*
ISBN 978-91-86287-75-7

Photo: Eliq Maranik and Stefan Lindström, except p. 20, iStockphoto
Art Director: Eliq Maranik
Layout: Eliq Maranik and Alan Maranik/Stevali Production
Editor: Eva Stjerne Ord & Form

© for the English edition: h.f.ullmann publishing GmbH
Special edition

Translation from Swedish: Casper Sare in association with First Edition Translations Ltd, Cambridge, UK
Coverphotos: Eliq Maranik and Stefan Lindström
Overall responsibility for production: h.f.ullmann publishing GmbH, Potsdam, Germany

Printed in Poland, 2016
ISBN 978-3-8480-0938-1
10 9 8 7 6 5 4 3 2 1
X IX VIII VII VI V IV III II I

www.ullmann-publishing.com
newsletter@ullmann-publshing.com
facebook.com/ullmann.social

The information and recipes printed in this book are
provided to the best of our knowledge and belief and
from our own experience. However neither the author
nor the publisher shall accept liability for any damage
whatsoever which may arise directly or indirectly
from the use of this book. This disclaimer applies in
particular to the use and consumption of untreated
raw milk and/or raw milk products, which the author
and publisher strongly advise against due to the
associated health risks.
It is advisable not to serve dishes that contain raw
eggs to very young children, pregnant women, elderly
people, or to anyone weakened by serious illness. If
in any doubt, consult your doctor. Be sure that all the
eggs you use are as fresh as possible.

Please note that bee pollen can be dangerous to those
with allergies to bees, their products or other seasonal
allergies.